# ENTERTAINMENT, EDUCATION, AND THE HARD SELL

## Three Decades of Network Children's Television

### Joseph Turow

PRAEGER

PRAEGER SPECIAL STUDIES • PRAEGER SCIENTIFIC

**Library of Congress Cataloging in Publication Data**

Turow, Joseph.
   Entertainment, education, and the hard sell.

   Includes bibliographical references and index.
   1.  Children's television programs—United States—
History and criticism.  I.  Title.
PN1992.8.C46T8   791.45'09'09352054     80-25162
ISBN 0-03-057704-7

Published in 1981 by Praeger Publishers
CBS Educational and Professional Publishing
A Division of CBS, Inc.
521 Fifth Avenue, New York, New York 10175 U.S.A.

Printed in the United States of America

# PREFACE

This is a study of series programming for children that appeared on the ABC, CBS, and NBC television networks from 1948 through 1978. The investigation began in early 1979, when the Children's Television Task Force of the Federal Communications Commission asked me to chart changes in certain aspects of commercial network television over time. The work proved fascinating. Particularly intriguing to me were the themes of "diversity" and the "shape" of children's television that echoed throughout our data. These themes had no direct bearing on the initial research purpose, but they were loaded with historical interest as well as with present and future policy implications. Therefore, after completing my work for the task force, I returned to the material, poured over biyearly series changes and continuities, tracked diversity and the shape of programming, placed them alongside developments in the television industry, and confronted the meaning of all of it. This book is the result.

There were many people to thank along the way. Susan Greene and Brian Fontes of the Federal Communications Commission instigated the initial research, thereby channeling my longtime interest in children's programming into a policy-oriented project. Edward Gaine and Maureen Delp, my research assistants, occupied themselves beyond the call of duty in many areas of the investigation. Sandy Wilson typed quickly and patiently. Robert Lewis Shayon supplied strong doses of sage advice. Lynda Sharp of Praeger provided editorial help and encouragement. Abraham and Danuta Turow, my parents, added their solid interest and support.

Judith Turow, my wife, has followed this work's progress on a daily basis, from start to finish. Her patience, good advice, and companionship have been invaluable. And I have dedicated this book to her.

# CONTENTS

# LIST OF TABLES AND FIGURES

# *1*
## INTRODUCTION

Television has no sign on it: "Trespassers will be prose-
cuted." Television is living made easy for our children.
It is the shortest cut yet devised, the most accessible back
door to the grown-up world. Television is never too busy
to talk to our children. Television plays with them, shares
its work with them. Television wants their attention, needs
it, goes to any length to get it.

Robert Lewis Shayon wrote these comments in an article for the
Saturday Review of Literature back in November 1950.[1] He called
the article "The Pied Piper of Video" and devoted it to an exploration
of the possible consequences the television medium was having on
U.S. youngsters. Television had been introduced commercially on a
large scale only a few years before, but the video pastime caught on
quickly. In 1947, 14,000 homes, or .04 percent of families in the
United States, owned television receivers. In 1948 the number of
homes with television sets jumped to 172,000, .4 percent of the families. Two years later, when "The Pied Piper of Video" was published,
the number was 3,875,000, or 9 percent of the family population. The
next year would see the number of homes with sets soar to 15.3 million—a full 23.5 percent of U.S. families.[2]
    Actually, during 1950 and 1951, many U.S. residents had little
incentive to buy television sets, since their areas could not receive
any signals. In 1948 the Federal Communications Commission (FCC),
the main broadcast regulatory body, had discovered important problems involving signal interference in its television frequency allocation activity and had declared a "freeze" on new licenses so that it
might resolve the problems. The freeze lasted three and a half years,
and, during that time (1948-52), significant areas of the country had
few, if any, video channels. Los Angeles and New York City did have

seven stations each. But such cities as Austin; Denver; Little Rock; Portland, Maine; and Portland, Oregon, had no stations at all.[3] Writing in 1950, Shayon knew that television was not a requirement, or even a possibility, for every home with a child. Yet he also recognized the growing strength and attractiveness of the electronic pied piper as it stood poised to move across the nation.

> It is possible, of course, to have normal, happy children
> in a TV-less home. However, child-study experts point
> out that there are weaknesses to this cutting-of-the-Gordian-
> knot method. The most obvious weakness is that no child
> today, even in rural areas, can really be isolated from tele-
> vision. TV grows more ubiquitous with each passing hour.
> If your child does not watch it at home, he will, sooner or
> later, see it at your neighbors, even at school, or else-
> where.[4]

Prophetic as these words appear, they also seem a bit outdated in suggesting that children would have to leave their homes in order to watch television. For, by 1977, about 71.5 million homes in the United States (98 percent of the total) had one or more receivers.[5] Children were found in about 17 percent of those homes, and they watched a lot of television.[6] In 1976, according to the Nielsen Television Index, boys and girls aged 11 and under viewed an average of 27.6 hours a week, an increase from the 23.5 hours a week children viewed in 1967.[7] However, it should be noted that, as a group, children in the 1970s were not extreme in their television viewing. While teens (aged 12 through 17) of both sexes and men aged 18 through 49 watched less than children did, women aged 18 through 49 and people aged 50 and over watched a good deal more.[8] Nevertheless, by the 1970s it was common for many parent, teacher, medical, and government groups interested in television to focus particularly on the medium's relationship with children. Underlying that tendency was a concern that the youngest in the population were most likely to be swayed by the electronic pied piper and its images. The premise these often disparate groups shared was well stated by Gerald Looney in 1971. "Television has become an integral part of the ecology of childhood and deserves the same concern and careful consideration that we give to other aspects of childhood."[9]

Of course, parent, teacher, medical, and government groups were not the only organizations concerned with the heavy viewing habits of children. The broadcasters themselves showed a strong interest in the child audience. Between 1948 and 1978, ABC, CBS, and NBC, chief conduits of commercial television programs in the United States, targeted 405 series to children. And, in fact, much of the disdain and the applause of television's critics was reserved for those programs. Their comments ranged from the specific to the general. For example, in 1954 the National Association for Better Radio and Television (NAFBRAT), surveying the television scene, deplored the fact that "crime programs for children are being produced in a volume of approximately four times greater than in 1951."[10] By contrast, in a 1979 overview of children's fare, New York Times television editor Les Brown described network children's fare as "a heavy diet of cheap, fast-paced, mind-numbing rubbish."[11]

Critical comments about children's television were also often in disagreement. For example, in the late 1950s, NAFBRAT said that "Heckle and Jeckle" was a "cartoon series of excellent quality," while the national Parent-Teacher Association (PTA) called it "just a heap of rubbish." To NAFBRAT evaluators, the "Pinky Lee Show" was "a child's burlesque show; excessive bad taste," while, to monitors from the American Council for Better Broadcasts, it was "suitable for children. Just plain funny."[12] Similar disagreements issued from other organizations and from the print media over the years. They showed the difficulty of defining quality in children's fare.

Issues presumably less slippery than "quality" also came to the fore of public debate. The subject of violence in all programming periodically convulsed pressure groups, regulatory bodies, and congressional committees in the 1950s, 1960s, and 1970s. Other subjects, such as the presence of advertising during children's shows, the absence of age-specific programming for juveniles, and the low level of diversity in children's programming, percolated in relative obscurity until 1968. In 1968 a pressure group called Action for Children's Television (ACT), based in Massachusetts, was founded. Gathering strength from across the country, the group began to voice demands, quite loudly, for major changes regarding advertising, age-specificity, and the level of diversity in programming for children.[13]

Over the years, cascading criticisms of children's television brought forth warnings to broadcasters from government investigatory and regulatory agencies. They resulted in agreements by broadcasters to change advertising approaches to children (though not to end advertising). The criticisms also ignited more research on the interactions of children with television and on the many-sided consequences of television on youngsters. They led to sociological research on children's television producers,[14] to studies on the economic nature and profitability of network and nonnetwork fare,[15] and to suggestions for improving children's programming.[16] The criticisms also encouraged analyses of certain aspects of children's television programming. In particular, violence on children's television was actively studied. Beginning in 1968, George Gerbner's charting of the ebb and flow of aggression and power on Saturday morning cartoons was the most prominent, and controversial, work on this subject.[17] In the 1970s the increasing public discussion of advertising on children's television prompted systematic analyses of commercials aimed at children. Some of the studies were supported by ACT.[18]

Interestingly, throughout all the debates and the regulatory admonishments, the subject of diversity, that is, the range of program choices aimed at children, received very little attention in terms of research. Some important, useful analyses were made of particular aspects of children's fare during particular seasons, generally out of concern for the portrayal of women or minorities.[19] Yet, these analyses provided isolated "snapshots." They were frozen in time. Each analysis used categories or definitions or interests that were at least somewhat different from previous studies, and so the studies provided no clear picture of changes and continuities in the range of program choices aimed at children through the years.

Certainly, the subject of diversity loomed large for pressure groups and policy makers, if not for researchers, in the 1970s. In 1974 the FCC noted broadcasters' "responsibility to provide diversified programming designed to meet the varied needs and interests of the child audience."[20] In that same year, the Family Guide to Children's Television, endorsed by ACT, lamented the narrow range of choice in terms of scheduling, subject matter, format, and characterization in children's programming. The Guide argued that "it is essential that a choice of programming alternatives be offered, no matter how high or low the ratings."[21] In 1978 the FCC reiterated its insistence that broadcasters were responsible for providing diversity in children's fare.[22] However, although a few partial studies of trends in programming for youngsters did exist,[23] in the late 1970s no detailed analysis of diversity in children's programming during the previous three decades was available.

The absence of such an analysis means that no standard of reference is available by which to judge the present against the past. Without systematically collected data, defenders and critics of children's television must necessarily bog down in impressionistic debate on crucial questions. Has diversity in scheduling, subject matter, formats, and character portrayal narrowed or broadened in recent years? When the networks claim they are responding to criticisms regarding diversity in their children's schedule, are those claims accurate? What years are the networks using for comparison, and how do their claims hold up against other years?

In answering these questions by placing memory of the past alongside the reality of the present, it is all too simple to slide into that most difficult of all intellectual quicksands, nostalgia. It is easy to believe that the programs one watched as a child involved more diversity in subject matter, format, and characterization than do today's series. It is easy to believe—but very difficult to show in the absence of historical analyses of programming for children.

The purpose of this book is to present one such analysis and to lay the groundwork for more. The study asks two basic questions. First, how much diversity in subject matter, format, and character protrayal did children's programming provide from 1948 through 1978? And second, what conclusions about the overall development of children's programming during these three decades can be drawn from examining changes and continuities in diversity?

Answering these questions requires following the various aspects of children's programming carefully over three decades. As will be seen, these three aspects did not always change at the same time, nor did they always move in the same direction of broadening or lessening diversity. In terms of diversity, no decade was indisputably the best of times or the worst of times. Across these periods, however, network programming for children did go through a clearly discernible evolution. Therefore, in addition to charting diversity, the following chapters will detail that evolution and explore its relation to program diversity. In addition, they will show that the contemporary "shape" of children's programming raises important questions of social policy that should be addressed, since new juvenile fare is used increasingly to whet parental appetites for cable, satellite, and subscription television technologies. First, however, some preliminaries about the study and its method must be addressed.

WHAT IS DIVERSITY?

An earlier sentence referred to diversity as "the range of program choices" in children's television. It might be appropriate here to examine the concept of diversity a bit more carefully and, in doing so, begin setting boundaries for the study. As Barry Litman has noted, it is useful to discuss the range of television programs in two ways—in terms of "vertical diversity" and "horizontal diversity."[24] Vertical diversity refers to the broadness or narrowness of choices within a program category as seen across all time periods. By contrast, horizontal diversity refers to the broadness or narrowness of choices within a particular program category during a particular time period. For example, discussing the vertical diversity in subject matter means examining the variety of subject choices on the three networks or within a single network. Discussing horizontal diversity in subject matter would mean doing the same thing in relation to a specific time period (such as Saturday morning).

The largest part of this investigation will deal with vertical diversity in children's programming taken as a whole. Individual networks will sometimes be singled out, and the spectrum of choice during particular time periods (especially Saturday morning) will sometimes receive attention. But the primary aim across the 31-year period will be to develop a most fundamental knowledge of this subject—an understanding of the general range of choice in children's television programming on all three commercial networks.

WHAT IS CHILDREN'S TELEVISION?

At this point, another major term—children's program—needs defining. Two approaches can be suggested, one audience-centered, the other production-centered. The audience-centered perspective is that any programs children watch are children's programs. A variation on this notion is that the phrase "children's television" labels those programs children watch most. It should be clear that if all programs children view were considered children's television, a study of children's television would have to include everything on the home tube. During the 1970s, audience surveys consistently showed at least some children viewing throughout the broadcast day. In fact, a 1976 survey found slightly under 5 percent of U.S. children aged 2 through 11 viewing at 1:00 A.M. The prime-time (7:00 P.M. to 11:00 P.M.) audience, composed of 6- to 11-year-olds, fell below 20 percent only after 10:30 P.M. Viewing by youngsters under 12 reached an average peak—over 50 percent of that population in front of the set—at 9:00 P.M. daily and between 8:00 A.M. and 11:00 A.M. on Saturdays.[25] In fact, if what children watch most were the criterion for a "children's show," the programs and the program types commanding attention would overlap with those their parents view in large number. Prime-time situation comedies and dramas would have to be included along with Saturday morning fare.

The problem with this perspective is that, in essence, children's television is determined by default. The definition is guided, to a large extent, by the coincidence of children's free viewing time with available network products. Such an approach is fine for the exploration of what children are watching. It will not do if, as in the case of this research, the ultimate goal is to help improve (or broaden) television programming designed for children. Espousing that goal means espousing the producer-centered approach. According to this view, singling out a children's show means focusing upon programs that the production firms and/or the networks specifically intended for children. Of course, the greatest difficulty in carrying out that task involves the determination of the intentions of television executives before or during the period in which the programs were aired. Asking contemporary network personnel to label past children's shows would not be a satisfactory approach. Their choices could not help but reveal as much about the problems of present-day broadcasting and public relations as about past children's shows.

As it happens, two sets of records exist that allow the pinpointing of programs the networks targeted specifically at children from 1948 through 1978. One set is the file of network publicity releases that ABC, CBS, and NBC generate when new programs are aired. Releases designate certain programs as intended especially for children and often describe the enjoyment the programs are expected to provide for youngsters. Anthony Maltese used these publicity releases to create a catalog of children's series on the three major commercial networks from 1948 through 1964.[26] In turn Maltese's catalog became an important basis for designating the children's shows in this study.

Because Maltese's work ends after 1964, another source was needed to bring the list of shows to 1978. The network publicity releases themselves (available in the Television Information Office Library) would certainly have served this need. However, an alternative vehicle was available that paralleled the "children's program" designations and provided access to that information more quickly and efficiently. This was the National Nielsen Television Index Report.[27]

To understand the utility of the Nielsen Index Report for labeling children's shows, it is first important to understand the role of the Nielsen ratings in the television industry. Commercial television is, foremost, a business. As Les Brown notes in his book on "the business behind the box," the guiding rationale for programming is that it provides audiences for advertisers.[28] In order to carry out this basic delivery task, some system of audience monitoring is needed. The A. C. Nielsen Company provides the major national audience-auditing service for the networks and their affiliates, although other firms, notably Arbitron, also sell audience-rating data. The basic mechanism that Nielsen currently uses in its national rating activity is a small box, an audimeter, which the firm attaches to television sets in a statistically random sample of about 1,200 households. The audimeters silently record the on/off and channel-switching habits of the "Nielsen families" throughout the day. Periodically, the information so noted is collected by the firm and analyzed. Audimeters in New York, Chicago, and Los Angeles feed directly into a computer to allow overnight retrieval of rating results.[29]

Statisticians do agree that a random sample of 1,200 households is sufficient to gauge the viewing habits of the U.S. population in an accurate manner. At the same time, the A. C. Nielsen Company has periodically been attacked by pressure groups, members of the public, and even members of Congress for alleged inaccuracies in its polling procedures. Some have charged that a significant percentage of the firm's audimeters are inoperative at any point in time and that

the lowered sample size has much lower probability of accurately paralleling the entire population's viewing habits.  Others have noted
that Nielsen has often had difficulty maintaining working audimeters
in poor neighborhoods and consequently cannot measure the television
interests of poor minority households accurately.  Still others have
questioned whether families that know they are "Nielsen families"
act differently from other U.S. residents simply because they know
they are setting a trend.[30]

Despite this controversy, the Nielsen rating reports are used
as primary programming scorecards by advertising, production, network, and broadcast station executives.  A report's announcement of
a show's rating (its audience score as a percentage of all potential
viewers in the United States), its share (its audience score as a percentage of the people watching television during its airing), and its
demographic breakout (most prominently, the sex and age of its viewers) are often crucial in network decisions regarding the show's sur-
vival and the cost of its commercial minutes.

What is most important for the purposes of this study, however,
is that the Nielsen reports contain program codes, designated by the
networks, that label the intended subject matter and/or audience of
the show.  Some of the codes have changed over the years.  In 1978
the Nielsen report offered 37 "program-type" categories:

| | |
|---|---|
| Adventure | Instructions and advice |
| Audience participation | Musical drama |
| Award ceremonies and pageants | News |
| Child day, animation | Official police |
| Child day, live | Political |
| Child evening | Popular music, contemporary |
| Child multiweekly | Popular music, standard |
| Comedy variety | Private detective |
| Concert music | Quiz, giveaway |
| Conversations and colloquies | Quiz, panel |
| Daytime drama | Science fiction |
| Devotional | Situation comedy |
| Documentary, general | Sports, anthology |
| Documentary, news | Sports, commentary |
| Evening animation | Sports event |
| Feature film | Suspense/mystery |
| Format varies | Unclassified |
| General drama | Western drama |
| General variety | |

These categories are undefined in the report, and they need not
be mutually exclusive.  (For example, cannot an official police story

also be an adventure program?) A Nielsen representative said the firm leaves to each network the task of pinning a label on each of its programs. He added that a network might choose a specific label for a show to encourage advertisers interested in particular program types or audiences to follow that program's performance. Noteworthy in this connection are the several labels for children's programs. Similar children's program classifications were traced back to 1959 in Nielsen ratings, though they were likely used even before then. A comparison between the Nielsen children's program labels and the shows cataloged by Maltese from 1959 through 1964 allowed a check on the reliability and validity of each source. No contradictions appeared. Consequently, the Nielsen labels were used with confidence as a guide to programs the networks intentionally oriented to children from 1965 through 1978.

## ANALYZING THE PROGRAMS

One decision that was made near the outset of the study was to focus on series programs for children, that is, on network programs appearing on a regular (although not nececessarily weekly) basis. Historically, the children's series was by far the dominant vehicle the commercial networks used to reach children.

Next came a decision on the aspects of the programs that should be analyzed. Here concern with public policy issues had to be tempered by a major practical limitation; that is, no repository of all three decades of children's series was (or is) in existence. It was therefore impossible to actually view all the shows. Consequently, the categories selected had to reflect knowledge that could be obtained clearly from other sources—the Maltese catalog, the Nielsen rating reports, newspaper and television guide listings, and published references to television programming. Fortunately, the material available was satisfactory for investigating certain aspects of diversity in scheduling, subject matter, format, and character portrayal. Particular questions about diversity in those areas of program content were developed from issues of public debate during the 1970s.

For example, during the past several years a major concern about the scheduling of children's programs has been the scarcity of programs televised by the networks on weekday afternoons, when children are away from school. In 1974 the Guide to Children's Television, endorsed by ACT, complained that "in 1971, the United States was the only major country where television networks did not carry weekday afternoon programs for children."[31] Certainly, memory and casual surveys of children's program history recall that there has not always been a dearth of afternoon fare. During what years were network children's series broadcast on weekday afternoons? How many afternoon series existed, and when did they begin to fade? In general, what has been the historic distribution of time periods for network children's programs? What was the period of greatest diversity in scheduling, and what was the period with least diversity? An aim of the research was to answer these and related questions.

The subject matter of children's series has also been an area of contention among those debating the merits and demerits of children's television. One recent concern has been the small number of nonfiction series. In 1979 the FCC lamented the scarcity of educational and informational programs for youngsters and urged networks to improve their performance on this score.[32] In a related area, ACT and other groups attacked the networks' tendency to serve large numbers of fantasy series to youngsters. They were also angry that only a very small number of programs "encourage active participation by children" and that many "new" children's shows are simply slightly changed versions of previous programs.[33] In this investigation, those contentions were placed in a historical frame of reference. The research focused on the main subject of every series, its dominant time orientation (contemporary, historical, mythical, and so forth), its attempt to involve youngsters at home regularly and explicitly in the program, and the original source for its title or main characters.

The format of children's shows has been attacked for reasons that complement the attacks on the subject matter of the series. The networks have been lambasted for the nearly exclusive use of animated fare that supports the fantasy thrust of the shows, for their reluctance to program series that take place in a studio and emphasize discussion or performance over frantic action, and for the absence of children (aged 11 or younger) in the continuing casts of children's shows.[34] Consequently, during this study, attention was paid to whether the series utilized animation, puppets, real people (live action), or a combination of these categories; whether the program was studio based, not studio based, or a combination; and whether children were included in the continuing cast.

Two aspects of characterization that were tracked related to the concern about too much fantasy. Attention was paid to whether the title character was endowed with superpowers and whether the continuing characters on the show were humans, real animals, or animals behaving as humans. Related to characterization was analysis aimed at shedding some historical light on a particularly vocal concern of the 1970s—the lack of diversity in sex roles, racial roles, and ethnic roles in children's series.[35] Unfortunately, detailed exploration of male, female, ethnic, and racial activities in juvenile fare from 1948 through 1978 was impossible. However, some idea of sexual, racial, and ethnic diversity could be obtained by noting whether the host and/or title character was male or female, whether the children in the continuing cast were male or female, and whether the program primarily revolved around a specifically defined ethnic or racial issue or environment.

The aspects of scheduling, subject matter, format, and characterization were defined carefully, so that two researchers, working independently and using a clearly defined data base, could note the information systematically. These coders were trained and tested for reliability. Their material was supplemented by more qualitative descriptions and evaluations of the children's series found in a variety of sources. As a result, the quantitatively based picture of diversity in children's television over the years received elaboration and texture. More detail on the methods used in this investigation is found in Appendix A.

This multifaceted exploration of diversity yielded a valuable dividend. Putting together the various categories as they appeared during each of the decades revealed that children's television developed a certain shape over the years. This shape could be described in terms of two broad dimensions—size and style. The size of programming refers to the general number of series, the duration of series, and the number of series that follow one another. The style is the combined approach to format, subject, and characterization at a particular point in time.

Therefore, in addition to detailing trends in diversity, this study will also chart how the various trends combined to move children's programming through a clearly discernible evolution in size and style from 1948 through 1978. Initially, children's programming followed radio's tradition of disconnected, live-action 15- or 30-minute series carried during the late afternoon and early dinner hours. By the late 1970s, children's programming had largely been shifted to Saturday morning and had developed into almost a mosaic of various interrelated long and short program forms. The pages that follow will detail this evolution, suggest some of the factors influencing it, explore its relationship to program diversity, and forecast its consequences for future children's programming.


A GLANCE AHEAD

Chapters 2, 3, and 4 explore trends in children's series by particular periods—1948-59, 1960-69, and 1970-78, respectively. Roughly speaking, these periods represent certain levels of diversity in children's programming and certain stages in the evolution of a contemporary "shape" to children's program fare. In an important sense, these chapters have parallel structures. Each chapter begins with an overview of the industrial and regulatory environment for children's programming during the period covered. Although a detailed history of the children's television industry has yet to be written, some fine outlines do exist, and they allow a sketching of the boundaries of programming acceptance confronting children's series producers and networks through the years. Following this overview are sections exploring the features of program scheduling, format, subject matter, and character portrayal during the period. Questions about vertical and horizontal diversity are explored. A final section recapitulates some major themes, ties the strands of the chapter together, and compares the findings with those of previous periods.

Chapter 5 will bring the findings of the entire investigation together and explore their implications for the present and future. Appendixes A, B, and C elaborate upon certain areas of the research covered elsewhere in the book. Appendix A is a more detailed explanation of the methodology, Appendix B is the coding instrument that was used, and Appendix C lists all the network children's series telecast during 1948-78—alphabetically and by two-year periods.

NOTES

1. Robert Lewis Shayon, "The Pied Piper of Video," Saturday Review of Literature 33 (November 25, 1950): 9.

2. Christopher H. Sterling and Timothy R. Haight, eds., The Mass Media: Aspen Institute Guide to Communication Industry Trends (New York: Praeger, 1978), p. 372.

3. Erik Barnouw, Tube of Plenty: The Evolution of American Television (New York: Oxford University Press, 1975), p. 372.

4. Shayon, "Pied Piper of Video," p. 50.

5. Sterling and Haight, Mass Media, p. 372.

6. George Comstock et al., Television and Human Behavior (New York: Columbia University Press, 1978), p. 91.

7. Ibid.

8. Ibid., p. 92.

9. Gerald Looney, "The Ecology of Childhood," in Action for Children's Television, ed. Evelyn Sarson (New York: Avon, 1971), p. 55.

10. Robert Lewis Shayon, "What's Good for the TV Child?" Saturday Review of Literature, vol. 37 (July 31, 1954).

11. Les Brown, "The Future of Children's Television," NCCT Forum 2 (Fall 1979): 9.

12. Shayon, "TV Child"; and Yale Roe, The Television Dilemma (New York: Hastings House, 1962), p. 73.

13. Barry Cole and Mal Oettinger, Reluctant Regulators (Reading, Mass.: Addison-Wesley, 1978), pp. 242-89.

14. Muriel Cantor, "The Role of the Producer in Choosing Children's Television Content," in Television and Social Behavior, ed. G. A. Comstock and E. Rubinstein (Washington, D.C.: Government Printing Office, 1972), 1: 259-89.

15. Alan Pearce, The Economics of Network Children's Television Programming (Washington, D.C.: Federal Communications Commission, 1972).

16. See, for example, Promise and Performance: ACT's Guide to TV Programming for Children, vol. 1, Children with Special Needs (Newton, Mass.: Action for Children's Television, 1977); Earle Barcus, Concerned Parents Speak Out on Children's Television (Newton, Mass.: Action for Children's Television, 1973); Evelyn Kaye, ed. The Family Guide to Children's Television (New York: Pantheon, 1974); and William Melody, Children's Television: The Economics of Exploitation (New Haven, Conn.: Yale University Press, 1973).

17. See, for example, George Gerbner, "Violence in Television Drama: Trends and Symbolic Functions," in Television and Social Behavior, ed. G. A. Comstock and E. Rubinstein, pp. 28-187 (Washington, D.C.: U.S. Government Printing Office, 1972); George Gerbner and Larry Gross, "Living with Television: The Violence Profile," Journal of Communication 26 (Spring 1976): 172-99; George Gerbner et al., "Cultural Indicators: Violence Profile," Journal of Communication 28 (Summer 1978): 176-207; and Horace Newcombe, "Assessing the Violence Profile Studies of Gerbner and Gross," Communication Research 5 (July 1978): 264-82.

18. For example, Earle Barcus, Saturday Children's Television: A Report of Television Programming and Advertising on Boston Commercial Television (Newton, Mass.: Action for Children's Television, 1971); Earle Barcus, Network Programming and Advertising in the Saturday Children's Hours: A June and November Comparison (Newton, Mass.: Action for Children's Television, 1972); and Ralph Jennings, Programming and Advertising Practices Directed at Children (Newton, Mass.: Action for Children's Television, 1971).

19. For example, Linda Busby, "Sex-Role Research on the Mass Media," Journal of Communication 25 (Autumn 1975): 107-32; Earle Barcus and Rachel Wolkin, Children's Television: An Analysis of Programming and Advertising (New York: Praeger, 1974); Gilbert Mendelson and Morrissa Young, Network Children's Programming: A Content Analysis of Black and Minority Treatment on Children's Television (Newton, Mass.: Action for Children's Television, 1972); Rita J. Simon and Michele L. Long, "The Roles and Statuses of Women on Children and Family TV Programs," Journalism Quarterly 49 (1972): 357-61; and Helen White Streicher, "The Girls in the Cartoons," Journal of Communication 24 (Spring 1974): 125-29.

20.  Federal Communications Commission, "Children's Television Programs: Report and Policy Statement," Federal Register 39 (November 6, 1974): 39397.

21.  Kaye, Guide to Children's Television, p. 48.

22.  Federal Communications Commission, "Children's Television Programming and Advertising Practices: Second Notice of Inquiry," Federal Register 43 (August 21, 1978): 37236-45.

23.  Maurice Shelby, Jr., "Children's Programming Trends on Network Television," Journal of Broadcasting 8 (1964): 247-54; and Anthony M. Maltese, "A Descriptive Study of Children's Programming on Major American Television Networks from 1950 through 1964" (Ph.D. diss., Ohio University, 1967).

24.  Barry Litman, "The Television Networks, Competition, and Program Diversity," Journal of Broadcasting 23 (Fall 1979): 393-409.

25.  Comstock et al., Television and Human Behavior, pp. 100-8.

26.  Maltese, "Children's Programming." Maltese's study actually begins with 1948.

27.  Nielsen Television Index Reports (Northbrook, Ill.: A. C. Nielsen Company, 1959-78).

28.  Les Brown, Television: The Business Behind the Box (New York: Harcourt Brace Jovanovich, 1971), pp. 49-50.

29.  Ibid., pp. 32-33; and Craig T. Norback and Peter G. Norback, The TV Guide Almanac (New York: Ballantine, 1980), pp. 70-75.

30.  Brown, Television, pp. 33-35; Comstock et al., Television and Human Behavior, pp. 86-88; and David Chagall, "Can You Believe the Ratings?" TV Guide, June 24, 1978, pp. 2-13.

31.  Kaye, Guide to Children's Television, p. 37.

32.  Federal Communications Commission, "Children's Television Programs," p. 39397; and Federal Communications Commission, "Children's Television Programming," p. 37238.

33.  Kaye, Guide to Children's Television, pp. 36, 50.

34.  Ibid., p. 48.

35.  Ibid., pp. 48, 51-55.

# 2
# THE EARLY YEARS, 1948-59

    Children's television was not created in a vacuum. The products of earlier media influenced program creation, as did the economics of television, the attitudes of sponsors, and concerns of organized public groups. Early children's programming was the product of a specific industrial and social context and that context set the boundaries for programming diversity from 1948 through 1959.

## THE LEGACY OF RADIO

    When broadcasters began to turn their commercial attentions to television in the late 1940s, they had the programming tradition of radio in back of them. A valuable way to explore that legacy and its implications for diversity in children's television is provided by Harrison Summers's detailed compilation of programs carried on the nationwide radio networks.[1] Unfortunately, since Summers does not rely on advertisers or networks for his program-subject categories, his listing of children's programs is not strictly comparable to the lists in this study. In addition, he fails to label as children's shows series that several other researchers indicate were indeed aimed at children. Specifically, what Summers calls "daytime thriller dramas," as distinct from "daytime children's programs," are described consistently as children's series by Erik Barnouw, John Dunning, Raymond Stedman, and others.[2] However, Summers's listing of network radio schedules, with the aid of other sources to designate and describe children's programs, allows some important insights into the diversity of children's radio at the dawn of children's television.
    Children's series appeared on network radio during the 1930 radio year in the form of two storytelling programs, "Lady Next

Door" (NBC Red network) and "Story Time" (CBS). * The first program, "sustained" without a sponsor, aired six times a week at 5:30 in the late afternoon for 25 minutes. The second show, fully sponsored by Book House, appeared at 5:45 P.M. three times a week for 15 minutes. The NBC Red program was gone the next year, but Book House expanded its show to 30 minutes, and Maltine sponsored a half-hourly "Story Time" over the NBC Blue network on Mondays at 4:00 P.M. In 1932 CBS, NBC Blue, and NBC Red carried a total of five storytelling programs, two of them including songs with a host and "gang" (a group of continuing characters). In addition, the networks set a scheduling pattern they followed for the next seven years. All of the series were positioned between 5:00 and 6:00 in the late afternoon, all were 15 minutes long, and all but one were aired either five or three times a week. Three of the five programs were fully sponsored; Summers says the other two were probably sustaining.

The next year, 1933, marked the height of children's storybook and storybook/variety programs on radio. The seven aired at that time declined to four a year later and to two a year after that. A low was reached in 1938, when only one show, Kellogg's "Singing Lady," was aired four times a week. While the next year also saw only one storybook series on weekdays ("Dorothy Gordon" on NBC Red), it did witness three such shows overall, since Mutual and NBC Blue each sustained a half hour on Saturday morning. That season set a new scheduling pattern. From 1940 through 1949, the networks aired no more than three storybook or storybook/variety series in a year. Moreover, of the six different storybook or storybook/variety series aired from 1940 through 1949, only one, NBC Blue's "Irene Wicker," aired on a weekday. The rest were positioned on Saturday morning or early Saturday afternoon. Significantly, "Irene Wicker" was a sustaining show, while three of the five Saturday series were fully sponsored.

What changes occurred to decrease the number of storybook and storybook/variety programs for children, reduce their frequency to once a week, and shift them to Saturday morning? Part of the answer lies in the rise of a very different kind of program aimed at children, the "daytime thriller drama." Seeds of change were broadcast as early as April 1931, when "Little Orphan Annie" took to the NBC Blue network's airwaves. The tyke in Harold Grey's popular comic strip

---

*From its formation in 1926 until 1943, the National Broadcasting Company owned two networks, NBC Red and NBC Blue. In 1943 under FCC edict, the firm sold NBC Blue, and the new owners named it the American Broadcasting Company (ABC) (Erik Barnouw, The Golden Web [New York: Oxford University Press, 1968], pp. 187-90).

thus helped establish the adventure program as the major radio vehicle for children. In addition, "Annie," together with NBC Red's "Skippy" that followed some months later, inaugurated the pattern for juvenile adventures that followed. The programs were 15 minutes long, aired six days a week around the early dinner hour, and utilized a cliff-hanging style.

Subsequent years saw many more such programs. In all, 28 children's "thriller dramas" were broadcast from 1931 through 1949. Although some of the shows were sustained by the networks, most were fully sponsored, often by cereal companies. Many of the program titles and characters were borrowed from newspaper comics, pulp magazines, movies, or juvenile novels. "Annie" revolved around a little girl, and some other early children's serials (such as "Bobby Benson" and "Robinson Crusoe, Jr.") had youngsters as title characters. However, the overwhelming majority of these programs centered around adult men. Shows about police or detective agents were common—for example, "Dick Tracy," "Jr. G Men," "Charlie Chan," and "Inspector White of Scotland Yard." Westerns were represented by such programs as "Bobby Benson's Adventures," "Tom Mix's Ralston Straightshooters," and "Cimmaron Tavern." Other shows had heroes circumnavigating the globe in search of action in different settings—for example, "Don Winslow and the Navy," "Captain Midnight," "Omar the Mystic," "Mandrake the Magician," and "Terry and the Pirates."

All the programs involved an action-filled fight against evil in one incarnation or another. The shows were aired more than once a week (usually three or five times) on weekday afternoons. As implied, they were not episodic series in which each broadcast told a self-contained story. Rather, their plots were "open-ended" and had suspenseful closings for each daily installment. Only when an adventure that had occupied the regular characters for weeks or months was completed did an episode end on a note of resolution. More often, a new mystery was introduced during the same episode in which the old one concluded. This "revolving plot" device was designed to draw juvenile listeners to the next installment.

The children's serials tumbled into the late afternoon period (generally 5:00 P.M. to 6:00 P.M.), attracted sponsors, and apparently garnered larger audiences than the storybook and variety shows. They displaced the latter, and, from 1939 through 1947, the networks used Saturday morning and early afternoon as a period for quieter children's fare. Most of the Saturday programs were of the storybook or storybook/variety type, though one hobby program and one quiz show—"Bright Idea Club" (NBC Red, 1939-41) and Dr. I.Q. Jr. (NBC Red, 1948)—were tried. In 1948 the networks injected some changes into Saturday programming and into children's fare generally. CBS and NBC placed two action dramas, "Adventurer's Club" and "Frank Merriwell," respectively, on Saturday morning. In addition, the half-hourly, complete-in-each-episode format of those shows was applied by ABC to two weekday afternoon serials—"Jack Armstrong" and "Sky King." The next few years saw an increase in the number of action-adventure series aired on Saturday morning as well as in the number of afternoon serials that "turned episodic."

Much remains to be learned about reasons for the developments outlined in the preceding paragraphs. What is clear is that they helped establish as primary children's fare adventure programs whose theme was law and order. There were very few storybook programs and shows with various performances, and even fewer programs of other types. Two periods had been staked out for children's fare—late weekday afternoon and, to a lesser degree, Saturday morning. The most common length for a children's show was 15 minutes, though 30 minutes was increasingly used in the late 1940s. A pattern of diversity had been set in children's radio programming. It remained to be seen which, if any, elements of that pattern television would adopt.


THE ECONOMIC AND SOCIAL ENVIRONMENT

The business activities of the major television networks in the late 1940s and early 1950s were guided, to an important degree, by the firms' experiences in radio. They realized that television had the same potential as radio for becoming an important advertising medium. Consequently, they spent millions of dollars in what was an unprofitable enterprise for the first few years, often drawing upon their radio profits for cash.[3] Their investment began to pay off rather quickly. In 1948 network and nonnetwork television advertising expenditures represented an insignificant percentage of advertising allocated among major mass media. By 1956, 20 percent of all major media advertising expenditures were allocated to television. The networks, in particular, did better every year. In 1950, before the FCC lifted its "freeze" on television licenses, 107 firms advertised on television networks (including the short-lived Dumont) and, in doing so, spent $85 million on network television. In 1952, as the freeze thawed, 197 firms spent $256 million on network television. In 1956 network advertisers numbered 321 and spent about $630 million.[4]

William Melody and Wendy Erlich argue that the first four years of commercial television represented a promotional phase. The networks' goal was to motivate families to buy a television set, and they considered specifically designed children's fare a valuable stimulus in that direction. As proof, the authors state that "it is noteworthy that during the early years of television, nearly half of the combined offerings for children were sustaining, i.e., presented without advertiser sponsorship."[5] Actually, as has been seen, a substantial percentage of children's radio programs had been sustaining, so the networks were following their own well-trodden path. Nevertheless, it is quite possible that ABC, CBS, and NBC wanted to place the most attractive programming possible in their new enterprise and that the inclusion of children's programs represented one move in that direction. In any event, it seems clear that, in later years, the networks expected their children's series to make money. In 1948-49, 6 (60 percent) of 10 children's shows were sustaining, while in 1958-59 only 3 (10 percent) of 28 children's shows were sustaining.

In developing television, NBC, CBS, and ABC borrowed another important practice from radio—the sponsorship and control of programs by advertisers. Throughout the 1950s, the great majority of sponsored programs were "fully" sponsored. Only toward the end of the decade did the idea of purchasing "participating" time for announcements between segments of a show (as opposed to controlling the entire show) begin to take hold. Under full sponsorship, the networks sold time periods to advertisers for prices reflecting the number of all potential viewers during that time. Since the number of potential adult viewers in the evening was greater than the number of potential child viewers, it made little economic sense for an advertiser who desired to telecast a program for children only to pay for "prime time." Therefore, sponsors followed the radio tradition of scheduling programs for children during the late afternoon hours.

The possibility of afternoon programming for children decreased after 1956, however, as the networks began to release the early evening period (about 4:30 P.M. to 7:00 P.M. New York time*) to their affiliates. Melody and Erlich attribute the progressive surrender of this time period to a change in perspective on the part of national advertisers. The success of "Disneyland" around that time convinced them that it might be more efficient to design programs for both chil-

---

*The program schedules in this book reflect the times the series aired in New York City. During the first few years of commercial television, coaxial cable lines and microwave installations were inadequate to allow the networks to reach all their affiliates simultaneously. Consequently, the networks made kinescope reproductions of the programs and sent them to affiliates unable to receive them by live transmission. This activity became unnecessary after 1951, when AT&T opened the first transcontinental television-network relay circuit (Max Wilk, The Golden Age of Television [New York: Dell, 1974], p. 212; and Sidney W. Head, Broadcasting in America [New York: Houghton Mifflin, 1972], p. 85).

dren and their parents, rather than for children alone.[6] In fact, a CBS executive admitted to TV Guide in 1958 that specific programs for children "are not resoundingly profitable because few advertisers want to specialize in this audience."[7] So, "assuming the costs of continuing to program for children [to be] higher than the presumed benefits," by the late 1950s, the networks had released the late afternoon time period (generally referred to as "the children's hour") to the local stations.[8]

It can be seen, then, that industry-related factors led to fewer scheduling choices for children's programs. To what extent might influences from outside the industry also have helped set guidelines for diversity or encouraged children's television programmers to make certain decisions about scheduling, format, subject matter, or characterization? Actually, the theme of diversity in children's programming was only a minor one in public debate. A desire for variety was generally only implied in outcries against violence in children's fare, which constituted the loudest criticism of the medium during the 1950s. Radio also provided a precedent in this area. Network officials were familiar with the rage expressed by parent-teacher groups and consumer organizations about the serial thrillers aimed at youngsters. Articles such as "Mothers Fighting Radio Bogies" in a 1933 issue of the American Mercury enumerated concerns about the effects those fantasy-laden, violence-filled daily adventures might have on children.[9]

Publicly expressed concerns about children's television took a while to work themselves up to this pitch, however. Maltese, surveying public criticism of children's television in the early 1960s, described its development in this way:

> In the early phase of television, the majority of com-
> mentators were concerned with the effects of television
> in general on children. Later, most critics found fault
> with the amount of violence and mediocrity of offerings.
> Criticism within the industry developed. Finally, gov-
> ernment pressure developed.[10]

Public indignation about violence in all television programming reached its height in the mid-1950s. Time and Newsweek publicized research that showed children's dramas as among the most violent on the air.[11] The National Association for Better Radio and Television said that "the amount of crime on children's television should dismay all parents."[12] Charges that television was instigating violence in youngsters were brought before a special Senate subcommittee headed by Estes Kefauver in 1952, 1954, and 1955. Among the subcommittee's recommendations in 1955 was a suggestion that the industry correct its programming.[13]

During the first year of the Kefauver hearings, the National Association of Broadcasters (NAB) had taken care to include a section entitled "Responsibility toward Children" in the first edition of its Television Code. In fact, the majority of that section dealt with limiting the portrayal of violence in "programs of all sorts which occur during the times of the day when children may normally be expected to have the opportunity to view television."[14] At the same time, the code explicitly justified some use of aggression on children's television. "Crime, violence, and sex, are a part of the world [children] will be called upon to meet, and a certain amount of proper presentation of such is helpful in orienting the child to his social surroundings."[15]

In the last year of the Senate hearings, NBC reacted to the negative comments about violence in children's television by setting up a children's program review committee, headed by Frances Horwich, star of the network's acclaimed "Ding Dong School." The committee, which included some academicians, offered a wide-ranging critique of NBC programs for children—that they were too violent, overexciting, and crude; that they contained bad grammar; that they overemphasized money; and that, in commercials, they presented toys as educational when they were not. Interestingly, one of the committee's recommendations implied that the network decrease violence by introducing more diversity into programming. It encouraged NBC to air additional "how to do it" shows, hobby material, folk music, and adventure programs "other than western and space material."[16]

These suggestions came just around the time advertisers were considering deserting children's programs for "family shows," and Melody suggests that rather than revise their shows for children, the networks and their sponsors simply reduced the number of such programs.[17] The NAB, for its part, reacted angrily to continued attacks on television. When Reader's Digest published an article in 1956 entitled "Let's Get Rid of Televiolence," an NAB officer called it "vicious."[18] That the association was, however, sensitive to the public attacks is indicated by certain alterations made in its Code at the end of the decade. The fifth edition removed the phrase openly justifying "a certain amount of proper presentation" of violence and sex in children's programs. In its place was a much softer declaration that "such subjects as violence and sex shall be presented without undue emphasis and only as required by plot development or character delineation."[19]

It is, perhaps, a reflection of the time in which the NAB's Television Code was produced that nothing in the section on "responsibility toward children" dealt clearly with the issue of diversity. The only implication that a wide variety of choices for children was desirable came in a statement that broadcasters should "exercise care" in affording "opportunities for cultural growth as well as for wholesome entertainment."[20]


## THE RANGE OF PROGRAMMING

The foregoing examination of industry and nonindustry influences on those who produced children's series from 1948 through 1959 suggested that radio's program tradition, the economics of sponsorship, and public outcries about violence helped set some boundaries for children's television choices during that period. It has been noted, in particular, that boundaries were set in terms of the scheduling of children's programs. The following sections will explore scheduling and other aspects of programming in detail, suggesting links between programming trends and environmental influences on producers. However, the major focus will be on the extent of vertical (and sometimes horizontal) diversity in scheduling and program duration, subject matter, format, and characterization—and on the overall shape of programming that these aspects of content combined to form.


Scheduling and Program Duration

The number of series and the amount of time devoted to children's programming sets limits on the amount of scheduling diversity possible. The greater the number of series and the amount of time, the greater the opportunities for a wide range of scheduling choices. Consequently, this section will begin by charting the number of children's series ABC, CBS, and NBC televised from 1948 through 1959 and the number of weekly hours the networks devoted to their shows. The discussion will then turn to scheduling and to a related area, program duration, and will examine diversity in program duration by noting the variety in program length that exists among series from 1948 through 1959, in two-year spans.* Diversity in scheduling will be analyzed by charting the variety of time and day combinations used to schedule programs and by assessing variety in the number of times programs aired during a week. Throughout, these three areas will be shown to be interrelated and to form a consistent picture of network programming for children from 1948 through 1959.

Table 2.1 charts the number of series the networks presented in two-year spans. Table 2.2 charts the number of weekly hours that

---

*The two-year span will remain the unit of analysis for this study. It allows for sensitivity to program changes and for more efficient display and comprehension of trends than does yearly tracking.

## TABLE 2.1

### Distribution of Children's Series by Networks, 1948-59
### (in percent)

|  | 1948-49 (N = 10) | 1950-51 (N = 52) | 1952-53 (N = 46) | 1954-55 (N = 41) | 1956-57 (N = 41) | 1958-59 (N = 28) |
|---|---|---|---|---|---|---|
| ABC | 20 | 39 | 32 | 32 | 22 | 36 |
| CBS | 30 | 25 | 35 | 34 | 39 | 32 |
| NBC | 50 | 36 | 33 | 32 | 39 | 32 |
| Total | 100 | 100 | 100 | 98 | 100 | 100 |

Note: Totals less than 100 percent are due to rounding error.

Source: Compiled by the author.

## TABLE 2.2

### Weekly Hours Taken Up by Children's Series, 1948-59

|  | 1948-49 | 1950-51 | 1952-53 | 1954-55 | 1956-57 | 1958-59 |
|---|---|---|---|---|---|---|
| ABC | 1.50 | 13.75 | 9.00 | 10.00 | 7.75 | 8.75 |
| CBS | 7.00 | 14.50 | 10.75 | 14.00 | 13.00 | 9.50 |
| NBC | 9.00 | 20.50 | 19.00 | 15.25 | 13.50 | 6.00 |
| Total | 17.50 | 48.75 | 38.75 | 39.25 | 34.25 | 24.25 |

Note: The table does not include series scheduled less than once a week.

Source: Compiled by the author.

the networks devoted to the series they telecast at least once a week. The first table shows that only ten children's series were broadcast by the networks during the first two years of commercial television. The number soared to 52 in 1950-51, declined a bit to 46 in 1952-53, dipped to 41 for both 1954-55 and 1956-57, and then dropped rather dramatically to 28 for the last two years of the decade. The amount of time devoted to children's series followed a fairly similar pattern. A low of 17.50 hours in 1948-49 was succeeded by a high of 48.75, a drop to 38.75, 39.25, and 34.25 for the next three two-year spans, and then by a drop to 24.25 hours in 1958-59. The three networks took turns presenting the largest number of children's series during the two-year spans. However, ABC consistently devoted the smallest number of weekly hours to juvenile series, while NBC tended to devote the largest number of weekly hours to its children's shows.

The general pattern of children's programming throughout the 1950s parallels quite nicely this chapter's earlier discussion of industry and nonindustry influences on the networks and sponsors. An initial tentativeness was followed by a surge of regular children's material as television's "promotional era" began in earnest. The leveling off in programming during the mid-1950s (represented by a greater reduction in weekly hours than in number of series) preceded a sharper drop in the series count at the decade's end, as advertisers deserted children's series for the seemingly greener pasture of "family programs."

That desertion was associated with the networks' gradual return of the early evening (4:30 P.M. to 7:00 P.M.) slot to their affiliates. And, in fact, the importance of the early evening as a vehicle for network children's series did drop sharply throughout the decade. In 1948-49 and 1950-51, 80 percent, then 60 percent, of all network children's series began in the early evening sometime during the week. In 1954-55 the figure dropped to 23 percent. The periods 1956-57 and 1958-59 saw late afternoon children's shows decline further, to 22 percent and then 19 percent of all juvenile series. Paralleling this decline was the rise of the morning slot. From 1948-49 through 1954-55 series starting between 7:00 A.M. and 11:30 A.M. climbed from 0 percent to 12 percent of the total, 28 percent of the total, and 33 percent of the total. In 1956-57 and 1958-59 the morning series represented 40 percent and 47 percent, respectively, of network children's fare.

Table 2.3 displays the various time and day combinations that the networks used from 1948-49 through 1958-59. It shows that the decrease in late afternoon children's series was not confined to any particular day or combination of days. Use of the early evening slot declined in "Monday through Friday" scheduling, other multiple-day placements, Saturday airings, and Sunday airings. At the same time

TABLE 2.3

Scheduling of Children's Programs, 1948-59
(in percent)

| | 1948–49 (N = 10) | 1950–51 (N = 52) | 1952–53 (N = 46) | 1954–55 (N = 41) | 1956–57 (N = 41) | 1958–59 (N = 28) |
|---|---|---|---|---|---|---|
| **Monday-Friday** | | | | | | |
| Morning (7:00–11:30) | 0 | 0 | 2 | 2 | 2 | 0 |
| Afternoon (12:00–4:00) | 0 | 0 | 0 | 0 | 0 | 0 |
| Early evening (4:30–7:00) | 30 | 19 | 11 | 7 | 5 | 4 |
| Prime time (7:00 P.M.–11:00 P.M.) | 20 | 4 | 0 | 5 | 2 | 4 |
| **Friday alone** | | | | | | |
| Morning | 0 | 0 | 0 | 2 | 0 | 0 |
| Afternoon | 0 | 0 | 0 | 0 | 0 | 0 |
| Early evening | 0 | 0 | 0 | 0 | 0 | 0 |
| Prime time | 0 | 2 | 0 | 2 | 2 | 7 |
| **One weekday (not Friday)** | | | | | | |
| Morning | 0 | 0 | 0 | 0 | 2 | 0 |
| Afternoon | 0 | 0 | 0 | 0 | 0 | 0 |
| Early evening | 0 | 0 | 2 | 2 | 2 | 7 |
| Prime time | 0 | 2 | 2 | 5 | 5 | 7 |
| **Two to four weekdays** | | | | | | |
| Morning | 0 | 0 | 2 | 0 | 0 | 0 |
| Afternoon | 0 | 0 | 2 | 2 | 0 | 0 |
| Early evening | 0 | 12 | 4 | 2 | 0 | 4 |
| Prime time | 0 | 2 | 4 | 2 | 0 | 0 |
| **Saturday** | | | | | | |
| Morning | 0 | 10 | 22 | 20 | 27 | 39 |
| Afternoon | 0 | 4 | 11 | 11 | 7 | 0 |
| Early evening | 10 | 6 | 4 | 0 | 2 | 0 |
| Prime time | 0 | 2 | 0 | 0 | 0 | 0 |
| **Sunday** | | | | | | |
| Morning | 0 | 2 | 0 | 5 | 5 | 4 |
| Afternoon | 0 | 4 | 11 | 10 | 10 | 7 |
| Early evening | 40 | 23 | 17 | 10 | 15 | 4 |
| Prime time | 0 | 2 | 2 | 2 | 5 | 4 |
| **One weekday and Saturday** | | | | | | |
| Morning/morning | 0 | 0 | 0 | 0 | 0 | 0 |
| Evening/morning | 0 | 0 | 0 | 2 | 0 | 0 |
| Other time combination | 0 | 0 | 0 | 0 | 0 | 0 |
| **One weekday and Sunday** | | | | | | |
| Morning/morning | 0 | 0 | 0 | 0 | 0 | 0 |
| Evening/morning | 0 | 0 | 0 | 0 | 2 | 0 |
| Other time combination | 0 | 0 | 0 | 0 | 0 | 0 |
| **Multiple weekday and Saturday** | | | | | | |
| Morning/morning | 0 | 0 | 0 | 2 | 2 | 4 |
| Evening/morning | 0 | 0 | 2 | 0 | 0 | 0 |
| Other time combination | 0 | 4 | 0 | 0 | 0 | 0 |
| **Multiple weekday and Sunday** | | | | | | |
| Morning/morning | 0 | 0 | 0 | 0 | 0 | 0 |
| Evening/morning | 0 | 0 | 0 | 0 | 0 | 0 |
| Other time combination | 0 | 0 | 0 | 2 | 0 | 0 |
| **Saturday and Sunday** | | | | | | |
| Morning/morning | 0 | 0 | 0 | 0 | 0 | 0 |
| Evening/morning | 0 | 0 | 0 | 0 | 0 | 0 |
| Other time combination | 0 | 0 | 0 | 2 | 2 | 0 |
| Total | 100 | 98 | 98 | 97 | 97 | 95 |
| Diversity index | .300 | .125 | .121 | .089 | .123 | .182 |

Note: Totals less than 100 percent are due to rounding error.

Source: Compiled by the author.

the table shows that the chief beneficiary of the increase in morning programs was Saturday. Children's series on Saturday morning increased from 0 percent in 1948-49 to 22 percent of the series in 1952-53, 20 percent in 1954-55, and 39 percent in 1958-59. In other words, Table 2.3 shows that, through the 1950s, a major scheduling shift occurred in the primary placement of children's series, namely, a shift from various late afternoon slots to Saturday morning.

That change was gradual, however, and many other scheduling combinations continued to exist. In fact, Table 2.3 indicates that the variety of time and day placements of children's shows increased throughout the first half of the 1950s from 4 scheduling combinations in 1948-49 to 15 in 1950-51 and 20 in 1954-55. The number of scheduling alternatives did decline in the second half of the decade (to 17 in 1956-57 and 12 in 1958-59) as weekday programming for children became rarer and as the overall number of shows declined. Nevertheless, it can be said that, in the 1950s, shows for children were mounted on every day of the week, in different combinations of days, and in virtually every time slot from morning to prime time. Of course, series were particularly numerous on weekends, and it is true that Saturday morning did take on increasing importance throughout the decade. However, the weekend's afternoon, evening, and prime-time slots also saw children's fare, particularly on Sunday.

Close inspection of Table 2.3 allows an accurate assessment of diversity in the time and day combinations used to schedule programs from 1948-49 through 1958-59. However, making comparisons of diversity can mean an unwieldy recitation of various numbers in order to indicate a greater or lesser range of choices. To facilitate a discussion of diversity with as few numbers as possible, and to gauge sensitively differences in diversity between two-year spans, an index of diversity can be calculated. This unit, also called the Herfindahl Index of Concentration, is determined by squaring the percentages of relevant categories (the time and day combinations in Table 2.3) and summing those numbers.[21] The resulting index will increase as the concentration of choices increases. In other words, the greater the diversity, the smaller the diversity index.

The utility of this summary measure can be gauged by noting that its rise and fall in Table 2.3 reflects the earlier discussion of diversity in time and day scheduling. The index falls consistently (indicating increased diversity), then rises a bit to its level of the early 1950s (indicating decreased diversity), and then rises more, though it does not reach the high of 1948-49. It should be stressed that, while the index is a useful comparative gauge, only detailed examination of the data can disclose the actual elements that make up the particular range of choices. Two distributions can sum to the same score and be very different in the nature of their diversity.

TABLE 2.4

Weekly Frequency of Children's Programs, 1948-59
(in percent)

|  | 1948-49 (N = 10) | 1950-51 (N = 52) | 1952-53 (N = 46) | 1954-55 (N = 41) | 1956-57 (N = 41) | 1958-59 (N = 28) |
|---|---|---|---|---|---|---|
| Less than once | 0 | 8 | 7 | 8 | 7 | 7 |
| Once | 50 | 52 | 65 | 70 | 79 | 76 |
| Twice | 0 | 2 | 4 | 2 | 0 | 3 |
| Three times | 0 | 4 | 4 | 0 | 0 | 0 |
| Four times | 0 | 8 | 0 | 0 | 0 | 0 |
| Five times | 40 | 25 | 17 | 16 | 10 | 10 |
| Six times | 10 | 2 | 2 | 5 | 5 | 3 |
| Total | 100 | 101 | 99 | 101 | 101 | 99 |
| Diversity index | .420 | .348 | .459 | .524 | .642 | .594 |

Note: Totals greater or less than 100 percent are due to round-ing error.

Source: Compiled by the author.

Thus far, this discussion has dealt with only one aspect of scheduling diversity—the range of time and day combinations. Table 2.3 provides insight into a second aspect of scheduling—the frequencies at which series aired during a week. Comparing 1950-51 with 1958-59 reveals that despite a similarity in the range of time and day combinations, the two-year spans were quite different in the number of times a week individual series aired. While 41 percent of the programs in 1950-51 aired more than once a week, only 16 percent of the programs in 1958-59 aired more than once a week. Table 2.3 indicates that the years linking 1950-51 with 1958-59 saw a progressive reduction in the number of series telecast several times a week.

Table 2.4 allows the investigation of this subject in much greater detail. The table's diversity index shows that, in terms of the frequencies at which programs aired during a week, substantially more diversity was present in 1950-51 than in 1948-49. After 1950-51, however, the diversity in program frequency declined sharply. Behind this decline was the movement of programs to a once-a-week schedule (generally on Saturday or Sunday). It is true that once-a-week airing always characterized the majority of children's programs on the television networks. However, the 50 percent and 52 percent majority of 1948-49 and 1950-51 gave way to overwhelming majorities of 65 percent, 70 percent, 79 percent, and 76 percent in the two-year spans that ended the decade. Eliminated by the onslaught of once-a-week series were shows that aired three times or four times a week. In 1958-59 only a few shows aired two or six times a week. The broadcasting of a program five times a week, as was frequently done on weekday mornings and late afternoons in the early 1950s, remained. However, this practice was much less common at the end of the decade.

One category of Table 2.4 that held steady—"less than once a week"—needs some explanation. The category includes programs that were purposefully broadcast on a nonweekly basis as well as weekly shows that aired for less than three months during a two-year span. Examples of the latter type are "Children's Corner" and "Choose Up Sides," both of which aired in 1956-57. The former type is more interesting. The early 1950s saw a number of programs alternating with other programs every second week. For example, "Magic Slate" alternated with "Quiz Kids" during part of its 1950-51 run, and "Junior Rodeo" rotated with "Sky King" during 1952-53. By the end of the decade, however, such alternating series disappeared. A new way to schedule children's series on a less than weekly basis was introduced in 1958-59, when CBS began to air its "Young People's Concerts" four times a year.

The movement of the great majority of children's programs to a once-a-week schedule during the 1950s was accompanied by a standardization of program length to a half hour. A half-hourly duration characterized 60 percent of the series in 1948-59 and 58 percent in 1950-51. Over subsequent two-year spans, half-hourly programs increased dramatically, to 70 percent, 79 percent, 88 percent, and 83 percent. During this rise, the hour-long show maintained a fairly steady, though small, hold on programming. It was the 15-minute program—the common length in children's radio—that was a clear casualty of the half hour's increased dominance. Shows lasting 15 minutes—11 of them appeared from 1948-49 through 1958-59—were likely to span several weekdays in the late afternoon. As the networks shifted their programming away from late afternoons, and as once-a-week, weekend programming became the norm, 15-minute programs virtually disappeared.

Figure 2.1 shows how the actual programming of network affiliates at the start and end of the 1950s reflected these changes in scheduling and program duration. The figure lists material telecast by the

FIGURE 2.1

Saturday Morning and Friday Early Evening Television, January 1950 and January 1959

|  | January 14, 1950 Saturday Morning |  | January 17, 1959 Saturday Morning |
|---|---|---|---|
|  |  | 7:00 | Sunrise Semester (CBS) to 8:00 |
|  |  |  | Modern Farmer (NBC) to 8:00 |
|  |  | 8:00 | Cartoon Festival (ABC) to 10:00 |
|  |  |  | Big Picture (CBS) to 8:30 |
|  |  |  | Howie and Gordon (NBC) to 8:30 |
|  |  | 8:30 | UN Review (CBS) to 8:45 |
|  | No Programming |  | Andy's Gang (NBC) to 9:00 |
|  |  | 8:45 | Laurel and Hardy (CBS) to 9:00 |
|  |  | 9:00 | On the Carousel (CBS) to 9:30 |
|  |  |  | Children's Theater (NBC) to 10:00 |
|  |  | 9:30 | Captain Kangaroo (CBS) to 10:30 |
|  |  | 10:00 | Howdy Doody (NBC) to 10:30 |
|  |  |  | Film (ABC) to 11:00 |
|  |  | 10:30 | Mighty Mouse (CBS) to 11:00 |
|  |  |  | Ruff and Ready (NBC) to 11:00 |
|  |  | 11:00 | Uncle Al Show (ABC) to 12:00 |
|  |  |  | Heckle and Jeckle (CBS) to 11:30 |
|  |  |  | Fury (NBC) to 11:30 |
|  |  | 11:30 | Robin Hood (CBS) to 12:00 |
|  |  |  | Circus Boy (NBC) to 12:00 |

|  | Friday, January 20, 1950 Early Evening |  | Friday, January 23, 1959 Early Evening |
|---|---|---|---|
| 4:30 | Vanity Fair (CBS) to 5:00 | 4:30 | American Bandstand (ABC) to 5:30 |
|  |  |  | Edge of Night (CBS) to 5:00 |
|  |  |  | County Fair (NBC) to 5:00 |
| 5:00 | Ted Steele Show (CBS) to 5:30 | 5:00 | Life of Riley (CBS) to 5:30 |
|  |  |  | Movie (NBC) to 6:30 |
|  |  |  | Mickey Mouse Club (ABC) to 6:00 |
| 5:15 | Judy Splinters (NBC) to 5:30 |  |  |
| 5:30 | Chuck Wagon (CBS) to 6:30 | 5:30 | Movie (CBS) to 7:00 |
|  | Howdy Doody (NBC) to 6:00 |  |  |
| 5:45 | Time for Reflection (ABC) to 5:55 |  |  |
| 5:55 | Camera Headlines (ABC) to 6:00 |  |  |
| 6:00 | Small Fry Club (ABC) to 6:30 | 6:00 | Little Rascals (ABC) to 6:30 |
|  | Children's Theater (NBC) to 6:30 |  |  |
| 6:30 | Magic Cottage (ABC) to 7:00 | 6:30 | Beulah (ABC) to 7:00 |
|  | Lucky Pup (CBS) to 6:45 |  | News (NBC) to 7:00 |
|  | Easy Does It (NBC) to 6:55 |  |  |
| 6:45 | Bob Howard Show (CBS) to 7:00 |  |  |
| 6:55 | Weatherman (NBC) to 7:00 |  |  |

Note: The underlined programs are network children's series. New York time is used.

Source: New York Times.

ABC, CBS, and NBC owned-and-operated stations in New York City
during January 1950 and January 1959. The focus is on Friday's
early evening slot and Saturday morning because the previous pages
have characterized Saturday mornings and weekday afternoons as wit-
nessing the most significant scheduling shifts during the decade. One
shift clearly reflected is the drop in late afternoon children's series
by the networks between 1950 and 1959. The figure indicates that while
four such shows (totaling two hours) were presented in 1950, only one
network children's series (a half hour) was telecast in the late afternoon in 1959. Note that the ABC affiliate did not carry any network
children's programs in January 1950. Weekday transmissions of
children's series by that network were still about a year away. However, in scheduling fare with such titles as "Small Fry Club" and
"Magic Cottage" during most of its late afternoon telecast, the ABC
station did show recognition that the late afternoon was predominantly
a children's period. Ironically, in 1959, the ABC affiliate was the
only one of the three to continue this tradition, following the network
"Mickey Mouse Club" with the nonnetwork "Little Rascals." The CBS
and NBC stations, by contrast, seemed to aim no fare, whether programmed by the network or not, at children.

Figure 2.1 also reflects a drop in the variety of program durations over the years. The late afternoon in 1950 saw three lengths
used by the networks for their children's shows—the quarter hour
(CBS's "Lucky Pup" and NBC's "Judy Splinters"), the half hour
(NBC's "Howdy Doody"), and the hour (CBS's "Chuck Wagon"). In
1959 the one late afternoon children's series and all but one of the
Saturday morning network shows for children fit the by then overwhelmingly common length of a half hour. The mention of Saturday
recalls the increase of network children's programming on Saturday
morning between the early and late 1950s. Reflecting this change, the
chart indicates that the Saturday morning in 1950 saw no programs at
all, while the Saturday morning in 1959 saw eight network children's
series between 8:30 and 12:00 for a total of 4.5 hours. Significantly,
in terms of future trends, the Saturday morning network shows were
surrounded, in many cases, by locally televised fare that also seemed
produced for children.

Subject Matter

Thus far, interest has focused primarily upon the role of number, scheduling, and duration in shaping the presence of network children's series from 1948-49 through 1958-59. Discussion will now
turn more to aspects of program content and the range of subject matter used in the programs. Aside from charting the main subjects,

TABLE 2.5

Main Subjects of Children's Series, 1948-59
(in percent)

| | 1948-49 (N = 10) | 1950-51 (N = 52) | 1952-53 (N = 46) | 1954-55 (N = 41) | 1956-57 (N = 41) | 1958-59 (N = 28) |
|---|---|---|---|---|---|---|
| **Fiction** | | | | | | |
| Storybook | 20 | 8 | 9 | 0 | 2 | 7 |
| Western | 20 | 24 | 23 | 16 | 24 | 21 |
| Police | 0 | 0 | 0 | 2 | 2 | 0 |
| Science fiction | 0 | 10 | 11 | 12 | 0 | 0 |
| Jungle or "wilds" | 0 | 0 | 0 | 0 | 0 | 0 |
| Other adventure | 10 | 10 | 4 | 9 | 14 | 13 |
| Adventure in different settings | 0 | 4 | 2 | 0 | 0 | 3 |
| Realistic problem drama | 0 | 0 | 0 | 0 | 0 | 0 |
| Unrelated dramatic sequences | 0 | 4 | 2 | 5 | 18 | 21 |
| **Nonfiction** | | | | | | |
| ABCs, arithmetic | 0 | 0 | 0 | 0 | 0 | 0 |
| History | 0 | 0 | 0 | 0 | 0 | 0 |
| Geography | 0 | 2 | 0 | 0 | 0 | 0 |
| Nature | 0 | 2 | 4 | 5 | 2 | 3 |
| Other physical science | 0 | 2 | 2 | 2 | 2 | 3 |
| Occupations | 0 | 0 | 2 | 0 | 0 | 0 |
| Biography | 0 | 0 | 0 | 0 | 0 | 0 |
| Religion | 0 | 0 | 0 | 2 | 0 | 0 |
| Mixture nonfiction | 0 | 2 | 4 | 11 | 10 | 3 |
| **Performing activities** | | | | | | |
| Child sports | 0 | 2 | 0 | 0 | 0 | 0 |
| Competitive games | 0 | 4 | 6 | 8 | 2 | 0 |
| Magic | 0 | 2 | 0 | 0 | 0 | 0 |
| Music | 0 | 0 | 0 | 0 | 0 | 3 |
| Various performances | 50 | 23 | 30 | 26 | 19 | 21 |
| Subject mixture | 0 | 0 | 0 | 2 | 2 | 3 |
| Total | 100 | 99 | 99 | 100 | 97 | 101 |
| Diversity index | .340 | .144 | .173 | .140 | .157 | .158 |

Note: Totals greater or less than 100 percent are due to rounding error.

Source: Compiled by the author.

fantasy/reality orientations, and time orientations of the series, the discussion will serve as a prelude to examining the manner in which subject matter and format combined in the presentation of action-adventure series throughout the decade.

Table 2.5 presents categories that describe the main subjects of network children's series from 1948-49 through 1958-59. Nine categories are subsumed under fiction, nine are under nonfiction, five are designated as "performing activities" (programs that emphasize human entertainment skills), and one category indicates series that clearly belong in all three camps. As it turns out, the greatest number of children's series in the decade belonged to the fiction category, though fiction's majority varied from a very dominant 60 percent or more at the start and end of the period to a slim majority of 51 percent and a plurality of 46 percent around the period's midpoint. Performing activities consistently occupied second place, though their presence diminished fairly consistently from 40 percent of the programs in 1948-49 to 24 percent in 1958-59. Nonfiction rose from 0 percent in 1948-49 to a high of 20 percent in 1954-55, then fell to 16 percent in 1956-57 and 11 percent at decade's end.

The diversity index of Table 2.5 is based on an assessment of all 24 categories in the table. As the index shows, the two-year span with the narrowest distribution of categories was 1948-49. Afterward, diversity rose quite a bit, then fell and rose in two-year cycles. Series emphasizing various kinds of performing activities (among them even fictional presentations) stood out with the highest percentages during most of the decade. Ideas for these programs were often borrowed from the circus, vaudeville, or children's radio shows. Examples were "Super Circus," a program of circus acts; "Howdy Doody," a fast-moving mixture of songs, puppetry, audience participation, and films; and "Smilin Ed's Gang," a television version of radio's mixture of dramatizations, talk, and comic skits.

Very different in theme, but close to (in fact, sometimes exceeding) "various performances" in number, was a fiction category, "westerns." Some westerns (for example, "Chuck Wagon," "Bar 5 Ranch," and "Gabby Hayes") used different cowboy heroes at different points in the series. The westerns that lasted longest on television focused on the exploits of a continuing cast of characters. Think of "The Lone Ranger," "The Roy Rogers Show," "The Gene Autry Show," "Wild Bill Hickok," and "Rin Tin Tin." These contained clear-cut "types" common to most cowboy tales in novels, films, and radio— the sidekick, the cherished horse or dog, the bad whites or Indians.

The only subject category that matched "various performances" and "westerns" in being consistently present throughout the decade was that of "other adventure." Series under this rubric involved the adventures of characters who were neither cowboys nor policemen.

An example from the early 1950s was "Lucky Pup," a puppet show about the anthropomorphic tribulations of the title's canine hero, who had inherited a million dollars from a deceased circus queen, only to be preyed upon by Foodini, an evil magician. Later "other adventures" were "Circus Boy," an action-filled series with a circus background, and "Captain Gallant of the Foreign Legion," the battle-filled tales of a foreign legion officer and his young friends.

Appearing in every two-year span but the first were series containing unrelated dramatic sequences. Several films with no connecting threads made up these shows. For example, "Mighty Mouse Playhouse" portrayed the adventures of the title character as well as the antics of lesser protagonists. The same was true for "The Heckle and Jeckle Cartoon Show" and "The Boing Boing Show." At the same time, some programs with unrelated segments had no heroes in the title—for example, "Cartoon Teletales," "Cowboy Playhouse," and "Barker Bill's Cartoons."

Other fiction categories were scattered across the two-year spans. Programs emphasizing "storybook" tales and legends ("The Singing Lady" and "Shirley Temple's Storybook," for example) appeared in every two-year span except 1954-55. Science fiction series (for example, "Rod Brown of the Rocket Rangers" and "Buck Rogers") comprised 10 to 12 percent of the total programs between 1950-51 and 1954-55, then disappeared. Series that concentrated on single stories, but not necessarily on episodes of the same stories each week, made up a small percentage of the fiction area. Examples were "Telecomics" and "NBC Comics," both of which presented several short-run serials. Only one show was a police adventure. "Captain Midnight," aired in 1954-55 and 1956-57, brought to television the popular radio tales of a leader in a secret U.S. government organization established to combat evil. Totally nonexistent from 1948-49 through 1958-59 were stories dealing with life in the jungle or "wilds" and series focusing on "realistic" (everyday, nonadventure) problems of children.

Nonfiction categories tended to be even more scattered than the fiction categories. One nonfiction label, "a mixture of nonfiction," was represented from 1950-51 through 1958-59. It reached its peak during the Kefauver-conscious years of 1954-55 and 1956-57 with such series as "Let's Take a Trip," which featured visits to various places and objects of interest; "Summer School," a series of lectures on different subjects for grade-school children; and "Excursion," which featured everything from discussions and performances of great literature to bodybuilding. Another nonfiction category found throughout the 1950s was "nature." Programs in this area generally dealt with animals. For example, "Animal Time" focused on a different animal each week, and "Zoo Parade" dealt with several wild animals on each broadcast. "Other physical science," designating programs that dealt with subjects other than nature, actually described only one program during the 1950s, "Watch Mr. Wizard." "Geography and current events" claimed one program, "Watch the World"; "religion" was the subject of one series, "Exploring God's World"; and "occupations" found a humorous information outlet through "In the Park," a puppet show.

Performing activities followed the same pattern as nonfiction. Programs involving mixtures of subjects saw the largest and most common percentages, while the other categories scattered throughout the decade. "Competitive games" described a good number of those scattered series. Typical was "Hail the Champ," which involved children in needle-in-haystack hunts, indoor obstacle courses, cup-balancing acts, and other such tasks. Rarer was the quiz format, but it existed in "It's a Hit" and "Giant Step." "Magic" and "sports" saw light in 1950-51. The magic show "Foodini the Great" combined (mostly unsuccessful) magic with puppet chicanery. The sports show "Kid Gloves" involved youngsters in short boxing matches. The one music program, "Young People's Concerts," had Leonard Bernstein discussing music and conducting the New York Philharmonic. Admittedly, that program could have been categorized as a mixture of performing activities and nonfiction. In fact, however, the only program to receive a crossover distinction was "Captain Kangaroo," a soft-toned mixture of fiction, nonfiction, and performing activities from its debut in 1954-55.

Nonfiction is by definition anchored to reality—that is, to subjects that are plausible in the world. Fiction and performing activities are not. Interestingly, around half of all programs involving performing activities combined fantasy and reality from 1948-49 through 1958-59. However, such mixed fare was always in the minority. During most of the period there was an emphasis on reality. At first, in 1948-49 and 1950-51, programming divided rather evenly between reality and fantasy. This rough balance reflected the presence of storybook shows, science fiction, and some nonpolice adventures on the fantasy side. Westerns, nonfiction, and some performing activities tended toward reality. In middecade, however, storybook and science fiction shows decreased in number, nonfiction programs rose in number, and reality programming captured a clear majority—55 percent as opposed to fantasy's 28 percent. Series with a reality orientation continued to increase in 1954-55, to 63 percent of the total, and again in 1956-57, to 64 percent. In 1958-59 reality shows did drop to 52 percent of the total. The fall reflects a decrease in nonfiction programs and a rise of programs with unrelated segments that centered around animals acting like humans ("Barker Bill's Cartoons," "The Heckle and Jeckle Show," and "Mighty Mouse Playhouse," for example).

In addition to being classified as either fantasy or reality, main subjects can be grouped according to their time settings. Generally, performing activities and nonfiction took place in the present. Science fiction ("Buck Rogers" and "Rod Brown," for example) was positioned in the future. Westerns tended to be placed in the historical past, although some shows (for example, "Roy Rogers" and "Sky King") used the western formula in the present. Storybook programs ("The Singing Lady" and "Shirley Temple's Storybook") tended to combine a narrator rooted firmly in the present with tales taking place in the historical or mythical past. In view of these tendencies, the rise of programming set in the present, from a clear majority of around 60 percent in 1948-49 and 1950-51 to an overwhelming majority of around 80 percent at decade's end, becomes understandable. The decline of storybook programs and science fiction fare eliminated many of the programs that did not take place around the time of production ("the present"). Interestingly, the present even characterized several fantasy programs introduced in the late 1950s. Such shows as "Mighty Mouse Playhouse," "The Heckle and Jeckle Show," and "Cartoon Comedies" took place in contemporary atmospheres despite their implausible plots. Mighty Mouse, for example, conducted his feats of bravery against the backdrop of a modern city, and "Casper the Friendly Ghost" (a key character in "Cartoon Comedies") gently haunted present-day domains.

It should be noted that a concern for reality and "the present" did not necessarily mean a concern with contemporary individual or social concerns. Very few of the series aired between 1948 and 1959 confronted children's everyday problems on a straightforward, realistic level. A moderate percentage of series (between 10 percent and 20 percent over the two-year spans) did attempt explicitly to involve children at home in the televised material. "Winky Dink and You" even urged children to "help" characters through ordeals (for example, by drawing a needed object on a special television screen). However, only one nonfiction show ("Kid Talk") dealt squarely with expressed concerns of youngsters. And none of the fiction series unfolded the problems of juveniles in a realistic, nonadventure setting. In an era that had barely become aware of the right of minorities to have their point of view represented in mainstream cultural material, it is not surprising that there were no children's series dealing with racial or ethnic themes. (Squarely in the middle of the 1950s, an adult series, "The Nat King Cole Show," received much viewer abuse and had difficulty finding sponsors because the star was black.) The only program that dealt in any depth with another culture was "Andy's Gang," which ran a serial called "Gunga: The Indian Boy." It told the adventures of Gunga and his friend Rama who performed hazardous missions for their leader, the Maharaja, in India.

Looking at subject matter from still another perspective leads to concern with action-adventure plot lines. "Action-adventure" stories are tales in which protagonists consistently pursue and battle evil in their environment. Such stories (in dime novel, film, magazine, or broadcast form) have often contained violence and have often incurred the wrath of parent and teacher groups—witness this chapter's earlier discussion of objections to radio's juvenile serials. From this standpoint, it is perhaps significant that the first three children's series presented by NBC, ABC, and CBS had no relation to the action-adventure programming then dominating children's radio. ABC's "Singing Lady" involved a hostess singing songs and telling stories from the Brothers Grimm or Hans Christian Andersen. NBC's "Howdy Doody" involved a mixture of puppetry, tale-telling, audience participation, and silent film comedies. CBS's "Lucky Pup" was a puppet show portraying the travails of the main character in a circus setting.

Actually, of all ten series telecast in 1948-49, only two ("Hopalong Cassidy" and "Chuck Wagon") presented action-adventure fare. "Super Circus" was a circus-based program supporting various performances. "Judy Splinters," "Children's Sketchbook," "Mr. I Magination," and "Kukla, Fran, and Ollie" presented stories or performances in ways that applied visual elements to the quieter kinds of children's radio shows, the kinds the networks had shifted to Saturday morning by the early 1940s. However, during the following two-year span, the number of action-adventures increased to 16 out of 52, or 31 percent of the total. After hovering at 33 percent and 32 percent of children's series in 1952-53 and 1954-55, action-adventures rose to 37 percent of the total in 1956-57, before dropping to 29 percent at decade's end.

By then, however, another action-filled plot line had assumed some importance among fiction series. The "comic chase," a chain of escape-capture(or near capture)-escape sequences, had developed as a key element in "Barker Bill's Cartoons" and "Cartoon Comedies" during 1952-53 and 1954-55. In 1956-57 "The Heckle and Jeckle Cartoon Show" had been the first network children's series of unrelated cartoons to be named after major participants in a comic chase. This development of the chase for children's television, and important changes in the presentation of action-adventure stories, had been related closely to changes in the formats of children's series during the decade.


Format


Two reasons can be suggested for the networks' avoidance of action-adventure series in 1948-49. One reason relates to public relations; the other relates to the economics of series formats. First, it was probably clear to network officials that, if a goal during television's promotional era was to encourage parents to buy receivers, the best incentive would be to provide programming similar to the most respectable of children's radio fare, not material that upset parent and teacher groups. Support for this suggestion comes from the atmosphere surrounding "Lucky Pup's" premier. The first episode was shown at 8:30 P.M. (rather than at 6:30 P.M., its time slot) "to encourage parents and teachers to form opinions and critically react to the program."[22]

Another explanation for the networks' early avoidance of action-adventure programming relates to program costs. While radio actioners could spirit their heroes to exotic locales by dint of imaginative sound effects, the television medium had to portray those locales through sets or actual terrain. Costs of programs in which the primary locale was a television studio (or a puppet theater within a studio) were much lower than costs for action-adventure shows. One comparison will provide a rough idea of the difference. "Mr. I Magination," a studio-based program of various performances, was budgeted at $6,000 for 30 minutes in 1950. By contrast, "Tom Corbett, Space Cadet," an action-adventure serial shot in a studio, cost $4,000 for 15 minutes in that year. And, in 1950, "The Gene Autry Show," a western filmed outdoors, was budgeted at $27,000 for a half hour.[23] Considering these differences, it seems probable that in television's earliest commercial years program executives felt that higher costs should be avoided in most children's shows, particularly if less expensive fare could win promotional kudos from society at large.

One reason for network hesitations regarding costs probably related to an initial lack of advertisers for children's series. The networks initially sustained six of the ten programs aired in 1948-49. This situation changed rather rapidly, however. In 1950-51 the networks sustained 24 (46 percent) of the 52 children's programs. By 1952-53 the sustaining shows dropped to 30 percent of the total, and, by 1958-59 only 10 percent of the programs were sustaining. The entry of advertisers into the children's television arena should not be taken as a signal that program costs could skyrocket, however. As Melody has noted, advertisers' interest in children's television derives from its efficiency, its "ability to reach a large number of child viewers at a relatively low cost per thousand."[24] Consequently, it can be presumed that advertisers, whether they were "full" sponsors (as most were in the 1950s) or "participating" sponsors, demanded programs that could attract youngsters from the competition on a cost-efficient basis.

Research has yet to demonstrate that these considerations of promotion and cost actually motivated individual program producers and sponsors toward certain kinds of children's series from 1948-49 through 1958-59. At the same time, the considerations do help explain aspects of format diversity during those years. For example, in view of the previous suggestions, it makes sense that a large percentage of children's series originated in one indoor location (a studio) during television's early years. Programs that took place wholly in a studio made up 60 percent of children's series in 1948-49, 62 percent in 1950-51, and 61 percent in 1952-53. Indoor programs dropped sharply thereafter—to 36 percent in 1954-55, 32 percent in 1956-57, and 21 percent in 1958-59. Programs using outdoor segments on a regular basis increased accordingly, to 64 percent in 1954-55, 68 percent in 1956-57, and 79 percent in 1958-59.

It should be noted that the preference for studio programming in the early 1950s did not deter some producers from mounting action-adventure series. A number of advertisers went to the expense of sponsoring such outdoor action series as "The Gene Autry Show" (supported by Wrigley Gum) and "The Roy Rogers Show" (supported by General Foods). Other firms (including the networks) supported action-adventures created on studio sets—for example, "Buck Rogers," "Atom Squad," and various incarnations of "Tom Corbett." "Tom Corbett" was mounted three times a week and "Atom Squad," five. Both shows also had plot lines that copied the serial form frequently used in children's radio.

Another attempt to apply the action-adventure plot line to television in a cost-efficient way was "NBC Comics," known in a somewhat different version as "Telecomics." Both series aired several times a week for 15 minutes in 1950-51. Four story lines were used at one time or another—"Space Barton," an interplanetary science fiction tale; "Kid Champion," a boxing story; "Danny March," the adventures of a youthful private eye; and "Johnny and Mr. Do-Right," a story emphasizing the learning experiences of a boy and his dog. The series used off-camera narrators, actors, and appropriate sound effects to bring life to sequences of still illustrations depicting the adventures.

A more common way of introducing action-adventure into children's television involved the use of old theatrical releases. In the case of "Commando Cody," a science fiction serial about the "Sky Marshall of the Universe," this simply meant finding a half-hour slot to air the Republic theatrical movies that had been made a few years earlier. In most other cases, the old movies (often westerns) were introduced by a host who spoke from a set compatible with the film's subject. In large part, shows like "The Gabby Hayes Show," "Cactus Jim," and "Bar 5 Ranch" were simply vehicles to introduce old films. Sometimes, the humor of continuing characters (a "gang," as in "Smilin' Ed's Gang" and "Andy's Gang") added a bit more flavor to the pre- and post-movie performances.

The hosting of old films probably served several important functions for children's television in the 1950s. The format provided the action—and often material with a record of attracting children—that sponsors wanted. At the same time, costs were lower than fully original action programming. The hosts provided a convenient way of bridging the different features and of carrying the show to a consistent length (30 minutes or an hour). Nor did it hurt that the host could elucidate moral lessons from the films, teach rope tricks, introduce famous guests, or exhort child viewers to behave. Such performances might assuage parents concerned about the quality (or violence) of the old theatricals.

The continued movement of children's programming out of the studio in the 1950s was accompanied by a fairly steady level of diversity in the presentation methods used to put across particular subject matter. Table 2.6 presents these methods, which cut across studio/nonstudio lines. The methods range from series with episodes of single, unhosted presentations (whether dramas or nonfiction), to series in which hosts introduce one or more presentations, to quiz and nonquiz competitions. As the table's diversity index indicates, 1948-49 witnessed the greatest concentration of presentation methods, with one category—hosted dramatic performances—describing 70 percent of the shows. The 1950s saw quite a bit more diversity, with 1956-57 showing a particularly wide spread. Most categories maintained fairly consistent percentages throughout the decade. Unhosted programs with single dramatic or nonfictional presentations made up the largest category after 1950-51, and shows with hosts introducing one or more dramatic or nonfictional presentation consistently comprised the next largest group during the second half of the decade. Although most of these had action-adventure or comic-chase plots, there were interesting exceptions. "Watch the World," for example, involved newsman John Cameron Swayze and family hosting a program of films and guests relating to current events.

In the first half of the 1950s, the second most popular presentation method was the "variety show," in which a host introduced various entertainment acts, but not regular dramatic presentations. A long-lasting example of this format was "Super Circus," on ABC from 1948-49 through 1956-57. Broadcast live on late Saturday afternoons from ABC's Civic Theater in Chicago, the program combined a regular host, band leader, and trio of clowns with different circus acts every week. Beginning in 1953 audience participation stunts (for example, a hunt for coins in a goldfish bowl) were included in the program. Among other series in this vein were "The Big Top" and "Acrobat Ranch." Variety shows with no circus motifs were also present throughout the decade. "Judy Splinters," hosted by a ventriloquist and her dummy, was an early example. The "Paul Win-

TABLE 2.6

Presentation Methods on Children's Series, 1948–59
(in percent)

| | 1948–49 (N = 10) | 1950–51 (N = 52) | 1952–53 (N = 46) | 1954–55 (N = 41) | 1956–57 (N = 41) | 1958–59 (N = 28) |
|---|---|---|---|---|---|---|
| Unhosted | | | | | | |
| Single drama* or nonfiction | 10 | 29 | 35 | 40 | 31 | 35 |
| Several dramas or nonfiction | 0 | 4 | 0 | 0 | 10 | 10 |
| Hosted | | | | | | |
| Host with gang, drama, or nonfiction | 0 | 2 | 6 | 7 | 7 | 7 |
| Host without gang, drama, or nonfiction | 70 | 37 | 30 | 21 | 19 | 24 |
| Talk show | 0 | 0 | 0 | 0 | 2 | 0 |
| Demonstration | 0 | 6 | 6 | 12 | 7 | 7 |
| Quiz show | 0 | 0 | 0 | 0 | 5 | 0 |
| Variety show (no regular drama) | 20 | 17 | 15 | 14 | 17 | 14 |
| Concert | 0 | 0 | 0 | 0 | 0 | 3 |
| Nonquiz competition | 0 | 6 | 6 | 7 | 2 | 0 |
| Other | 0 | 0 | 0 | 0 | 0 | 0 |
| Total | 100 | 101 | 98 | 101 | 100 | 100 |
| Diversity index | .540 | .270 | .246 | .247 | .184 | .220 |

*Drama includes any performance that tells a story, whether live or recorded, studio or nonstudio based.

Note: Totals greater or less than 100 percent are due to rounding error.

Source: Compiled by the author.

chell Show," hosted by a ventriloquist and his dummy, appeared later in the 1950s.

Presentation methods seen less consistently than the variety format during the 1950s included the talk show, the demonstration show (where the emphasis was on showing how objects are made, used, or operate), the concert, the quiz show, and the nonquiz competition. Nonquiz competitions ranged from the relatively staid "Mary Hartline Show," which used games to act out such civic lessons as the way police act on duty, to "M&M's Candy Carnival," which used the circus environment of many variety shows to mount a talent search for the best amateur performer under 18 years of age, to the more frenetic "Hail the Champ" and "Kid Gloves," which have already been described. The decade's two quiz shows also had strong elements of excitement. "It's a Hit" used a baseball diamond and a mechanical baseball game to add action to a knowledge competition between two teams. "Giant Step" followed the example of popular adult quiz shows (for example, "$64,000 Question" and "Twenty-One"). The weekly winner could compete for seven weeks. If, at the end of those weeks, certain questions were correctly answered, the child won a college education and a trip around the world.

The talk show, concert, and demonstration formats were much less tension-filled. Only one talk show and one concert appeared. "Talk Around" had host Catherine Copeland encouraging children aged 10 through 14 to discuss their ideas about life. "Young People's Concerts" has already been described. Each program (and thus each format) appeared during only one two-year span in the 1950s. The demonstration format aired more consistently, primarily because of three long-lasting series—"Watch Mr. Wizard," "Ding Dong School," and "Let's Take a Trip." "Mr. Wizard," the series in which Don Herbert demonstrated physical, chemical, and biological phenomena for a youngster, began on NBC in 1950-51 and continued into the next decade. "Ding Dong School" aired on NBC from 1952-53 through 1956-57. In the program, "Miss Frances" Horwich demonstrated nursery school activities for her viewers—how to make clay figures, simple drawings, and cutouts; how to help seeds grow into plants; and the like. "Let's Take a Trip" took Sonny Fox and two youngsters to the Truman Library, the Lincoln Tunnel, the Edison Laboratory National Monument, and other places from 1954-55 through 1958-59 on CBS.

As the foregoing discussion indicates, the talk show, concert, and demonstration programs during the 1950s used a "live-action" approach to characters (that is, real people were used). While this approach was not so exclusively utilized in the variety shows and dramatic presentations, live action did characterize a majority of the programs aired from 1948-49 through 1958-59. Table 2.7 shows that

TABLE 2.7

Live Action/Animation/Puppetry in Children's Series, 1948-59
(in percent)

|  | 1948-49 (N = 10) | 1950-51 (N = 52) | 1952-53 (N = 46) | 1954-55 (N = 41) | 1956-57 (N = 41) | 1958-59 (N = 28) |
|---|---|---|---|---|---|---|
| Live action | 50 | 62 | 70 | 72 | 62 | 55 |
| Puppetry | 20 | 14 | 11 | 8 | 2 | 3 |
| Animation | 0 | 6 | 0 | 2 | 10 | 14 |
| Live and pup- petry | 20 | 8 | 9 | 9 | 7 | 3 |
| Live and ani- mation | 0 | 6 | 4 | 5 | 12 | 10 |
| All three | 10 | 4 | 4 | 7 | 7 | 14 |
| Other | 0 | 2 | 2 | 0 | 0 | 0 |
| Total | 100 | 102 | 100 | 103 | 100 | 99 |
| Diversity index | .340 | .419 | .513 | .540 | .419 | .353 |

Note: Totals greater or less than 100 percent are due to round-ing error.

Source: Compiled by the author.

changes in the use of live action across the two-year spans were sym-metrical. Starting at 52 percent of the total in 1948-49, the use of only live action rose to 62, 70, and 72 percent and then fell to 62 per-cent and 50 percent at decade's end. However, the categories offset-ting live action in 1956-57 and 1958-59 were not the same as those offsetting live action during 1948-49 and 1950-51. During the earlier years, puppetry alone formed the second-largest category in the live-action/animation/puppetry triumverate. By the end of the decade, however, the percentage of "animation alone" far exceeded that of "puppetry alone." This increase, and the fact that some "puppetry with live action" did remain in 1958-59, provided a spread of live-action/animation/puppetry categories that was more evenly distributed than during any other two-year span in the 1950s, as the diversity in-dex indicates.

At the same time, the decrease of puppet shows and the increase of animation toward the end of the decade upset a rough balance of pacing among network children's series. The action and breadth of activity in a live-action program (particularly one using a nonstudio setting) could never be matched in the constrained environment of the puppet theater. Consequently, the tempo of puppet fiction was slower and the tone softer than were the tempo and tone of its live-action counterpart. By contrast, sophisticated animations could place characters in any situation and speed them through activities at paces even faster than the quick tempo often used in live-action adventure series.

One important reason for the very small number of animated series during the late 1940s and early 1950s was that the most prominent animation units were controlled by the major movie studios, and they were loath to antagonize their exhibitors by releasing cartoons to television.[25] Hollywood-like animation required substantial investments and well-trained animators, and the networks did not try to copy the techniques. In fact, the few cartoon series initially aired by the networks were more like comic strips than cartoons. "Cartoon Teletales" (ABC, 1950-51) had Jack Lucksinger narrate stories while his brother Chuck drew illustrations to accompany them. "NBC Comics" and "Telecomics" (NBC, 1950-51) told stories through sequences of still illustrations backed by voices and sound effects. A most imaginative use of this approach was "Winky Dink and You" (CBS, 1954-55 and 1956-57), the center of which was an adventure told through a series of cartoon drawings. When a character was in trouble (for example, when Homer the pigeon was caught in a rainstorm), viewers were invited to aid it by drawing the essential item (an umbrella) on special screens applied to their television sets.

The barrier to animated reruns from the theaters was breached in 1953, when the William Esty advertising agency and its client, General Mills, bought television rights to the products of Terrytoons. That successful independent animation firm, based in New York, agreed to let its cartoons air in a hosted series on CBS, "Barker Bill's Cartoons." To avoid antagonizing movie exhibitors, the Terrytoons label was deleted from the televised material. However, concern about such antagonism grew progressively less important as the popularity of "Barker Bill" encouraged the airing of more cartoon programs. Cartoons were no longer popular among exhibitors, and, by 1954, financially ailing Hollywood studios like Paramount and Warner Brothers were selling their cartoon libraries to packagers who, in turn, were only too happy to rent them to the network or advertisers. Consequently, in early 1954, ABC aired "Cartoon Comedies," a Sunday series of animated shorts hosted by Paul Winchell. The films (which included "Casper the Friendly Ghost") had been created by Paramount Picture animators and had been distributed to movie theaters after World War II.

Neither "Cartoon Comedies" nor "Barker Bill's Cartoons" aired beyond 1954-55. However, CBS, realizing the potential lucrativeness of cartoon reruns, decided to gain control of a library and purchased Terrytoons in 1955. For the 1956 television year, the network inaugurated a new series of old Terrytoon theatricals, this time named after an already well-known Terrytoon hero, "Mighty Mouse." Mighty Mouse served as the show's host (through animated segments created for television) and introduced other Terrytoon characters. Terrytoon animators also created a new animated character, "Tom Terrific," for CBS's "Captain Kangaroo" series. A year later, a pair of Terrytoon characters, "Heckel and Jeckel," began their own run, using the "Mighty Mouse" approach. A few months after that, CBS began another all-animation series, "The Boing Boing Show," comprised of old United Productions of America (UPA) shorts. ABC entered the fray with "The Mickey Mouse Club," a combination of new segments and old Disney animations, and with "Woody Woodpecker," a series of old cartoon theatricals introduced by the title character's creator, Walter Lantz. Also around this time, NBC began to highlight cartoon characters in two program titles, "Gumby" and "Ruff and Ready." Neither character had seen movie screens. "Gumby" was the clay hero in stop-action animation adventures originally created for "Howdy Doody." "Ruff and Ready," created for the network by ex-MGM animators William Hanna and Joseph Barbera, detailed the adventures of Ruff the dog and Ready the cat as "they unite to battle the sinister forces of evil."

By the late 1950s, then, live-action adventures had been joined by adventures (and action-filled comic chases) in animated form. Quieter alternatives to action and adventure became harder to find on the networks, particularly in the main time slots for children. The program schedules in Figure 2.1 serve as examples. The early evening slot in 1950 was fairly well balanced in terms of pace. The gentlest shows were "Judy Splinters," a program incorporating live action and puppetry, and "Lucky Pup," a series using only puppets. Middle ground was occupied by "Howdy Doody," a somewhat frenetic combination of puppetry, studio and nonstudio live action, and animation. The other extreme was "Chuck Wagon," a series presenting nonstudio westerns.

By contrast, Saturday morning in 1959 was filled with fast-paced excitement. "Captain Kangaroo" did set a deliberately soft tone with its combination of live action, puppetry, and animation. However, "Andy Gang's" combined studio-based shenanigans with a nonstudio, live-action adventure about a boy on the Indian subcontinent, and "Howdy Doody" complemented its studio presentations in the late 1950s with live-action or animated adventure segments. Adventure also characterized the five other network children's series. "Circus Boy" and "Fury" were live-action adventures that often placed their child heroes in jeopardy; "Ruff and Ready" was an animated program featuring dog and cat adventures; "The Heckle and Jeckle Cartoon Show" contained action-filled comic-chase segments; and "Mighty Mouse Playhouse" combined comic-chase sequences with action-adventure segments.

## Characterization

The increase in action-adventure series and other action-filled programs during the late 1950s was accompanied by an increase in series with male title characters or hosts. Actually, the number of male headliners was always quite a bit higher than the number of female headliners. At their lowest period, 1948-49, men were the hosts or title characters in 50 percent of the programs, while women headlined 30 percent of the shows, and men and women together headlined 20 percent. In 1950-51, 14 percent of the series had no hosts or title characters, and this percentage remained fairly consistent throughout the decade. However, the percentage of female headliners decreased sharply from 1948-49—to 14 percent in 1950-51 and 4 percent, 5 percent, 7 percent, and 7 percent over the decade's two-year spans. Shows with male and female hosts or title characters decreased as well—to 6 percent in 1950, 9 percent in 1954-55, and 3 percent in 1958-59. At the same time, the proportion of shows with males as hosts or title characters jumped sharply—to 67 percent in 1950-51 and 76 percent throughout most of the decade.

A list of some enduring action-adventures of the decade illustrates that they comprised a male domain—"Hopalong Cassidy," "The Lone Ranger," "Gene Autry," "Tom Corbett," and "Sky King." Even when women were continuing characters in such series (for example, wife Dale Evans in "The Roy Rogers Show" or niece Penny in "Sky King"), they did not get top billing. The programs women hosted or titled were the quieter ones—the storybook shows ("The Singing Lady" and "Shirley Temple's Storybook"), the gentler variety shows ("Kukla, Fran, and Ollie"), the less frenetic nonquiz competitions ("Mary Hartline Show"), and the nursery school demonstration show ("Ding Dong School").

Males were not quite as predominant in terms of the percentages of boys and girls in the programs. (For this analysis, the term children is being defined rather loosely to include all minors, including teenagers.) The majority of programs had no youngsters at all in the continuing cast. That majority ranged from 52 percent to 75 percent between 1948-49 and 1956-57, then dropped to 52 percent in the last two spans of the decade. When a child did appear (generally in between 25 and 40 percent of the series), about half the time he or she was joined by a child of the opposite sex. However, when only children of one sex appeared, they were very likely to be boys. From 1948-49 through 1958-59, only two periods (1950-51 and 1958-59) saw shows with girls but not boys in the continuing casts. In all, only four programs (two in each period) used girls but not boys—"Panhandle Pete and Jennifer," "Judy Splinters" (where dummy Shirley was supposed to be Judy's younger sister), "Sky King" (with niece Penny), and "Susan's Show" (in which the title youngster traveled to a fantasyland by means of a magic kitchen chair).

Whether male or female, humans in general were overwhelmingly present in the children's series between 1948 and 1959. Shows like "Lucky Pup" and "The Heckle and Jeckle Cartoon Show," which had no humans in central continuing roles, made up fewer than 7 percent of the shows during any two-year period. The early 1950s saw the greatest percentage of series with only humans in the continuing cast— around 75 percent from 1950-51 to 1954-55. In the late 1950s, the proportion of shows with only humans dropped to 60 percent, then 50 percent, and series mixing humans and nonhumans increased accordingly. Particularly helpful in raising the diversity of character types were programs in which humans and animals together played central roles. Such series as "Rin Tin Tin," "Fury," and "Circus Boy" (with Bimbo the baby elephant) comprised 14 percent of the programs in 1956-57 and 24 percent of the programs in 1958-59, after earlier comprising fewer than 10 percent of the shows. Interestingly, the percentage of shows portraying humans with creatures behaving like humans remained fairly steady throughout the two-year spans separating 1948 and 1959. After a high of 20 percent in 1948-49, shows with this character mix made up between 14 and 19 percent of the shows throughout the decade. It should be noted that this steady rate belies an important change in the nature of the nonhumans that appeared. During the first several years of commercial television, they tended to be puppets (as in "Judy Splinters" and "Kukla, Fran, and Ollie"). By contrast, in the latter part of the 1950s, they tended to be animated animals in fantasy-filled cartoons (recall "The Mickey Mouse Club" and "Woody Woodpecker").

Fantasy images often evoke images of superheroes. It warrants stressing, then, that very few of the title characters between 1948-49 and 1958-59 had superpowers. From 1948-49 through 1952-53, only "Mr. I Magination" exhibited a kind of superpower—the ability to make anything come true through imagination. Later in the decade, two title characters used superpowers—Gumby (who could multiply, divide, stretch, or contract himself to any size) and Mighty Mouse (who gained incredible strength to fight villainy by eating supermarket foods). It is difficult to suggest reasons for such a small number of series with superheroes, although the strong presence of live-action programming (making special effects difficult or expensive) might be a factor.

THE SHAPE OF PROGRAMMING

The previous pages have taken a close look at various aspects of children's series and have attempted to chart the changes and continuities of those aspects from 1948 through 1959. Stepping back a bit, in an attempt to get an idea of the "size" and "style" of the programming during those 12 years, one general conclusion stands out. These early years of commercial television were years of flux. For reasons that have not as yet been found out, the size and style of children's television did not settle down quickly to easily reducible terms. It seems as if sponsors and networks used a good portion of the decade to search for the time period, length, frequency, and kind of programming that would be most efficient for reaching youngsters.

The suggestion that economic efficiency was a primary criterion in the search for efficient programming is supported by the finding that the greatest programming fluctuations related to the areas most tied to costs—scheduling and formats. In these areas and others, certain aspects of radio's legacy were tried and discarded—the daily program, the weekday program in the late afternoon, the 15-minute show, and the serial. Other features of children's radio were tried and kept —Saturday morning programming, the 30-minute show, the action-adventure series, and the storybook programs with various other performances. Nonfiction, never common in children's radio, was not common on children's television either, although it did increase slightly when Congress investigated television violence in the mid-1950s. Programs with performance activities maintained a strong presence, but fiction was dominant.

Action in various forms of fiction was stressed in different years. In the earliest part of the decade, emphasis was on old live-action movies. Later years saw producers turn to theatrical animation for their fare. Even the new material that was presented differed in form throughout the decade. The first half of the 1950s saw in-studio, live-action dramas and primitive cartoon techniques, while, in the late 1950s, those forms disappeared in favor of nonstudio action-adventures and Hollywood-like animation. It is true that even the "new" material and the "old" shared some important plot elements and characterizations. Certainly, the series paid virtually no attention to minority racial or ethnic groups. Title characters in the overwhelming majority of programs were males. Children were absent from most of the programs. Carrying the uniformity of characterization further, it is interesting to note that humans were central continuing characters in an overwhelming number of programs. Shows with "humans only" comprised a strong majority from 1948 through 1959.

This quite uniform approach to characterization not withstanding, the shifting scheduling patterns and formats make it difficult to define a consistent overall "shape" for children's television in the 1950s. However, looking back from the 1960s, it can be seen that a shape for programming was beginning to emerge at the end of television's "early years." The general directions programming took between 1960 and 1969 are subjects for the next chapter.

NOTES

1. Harrison Summers, ed., A Thirty Year History of Programs Carried on National Radio Networks in the United States, 1926-1956 (Columbus: Ohio State University, 1958).

2. Erik Barnouw, A Tower in Babel (New York: Oxford University Press, 1966); John Dunning, Tune in Yesterday: Old Time Radio, 1925-1976 (Englewood Cliffs, N.J.: Prentice-Hall, 1976); and Raymond Stedman, The Serials (Norman: University of Oklahoma Press, 1971).

3. Erik Barnouw, The Golden Web (New York: Oxford University Press, 1968), pp. 244-45.

4. Leo Bogart, The Age of Television, 3d ed. (New York: Unger, 1972), pp. 189, 193.

5. William Melody, Children's Television: The Economics of Exploitation (New Haven, Conn.: Yale University Press, 1973), p. 36. Melody wrote that chapter with Wendy Erlich.

6. Ibid., p. 44.

7. TV Guide, January 18, 1958, p. 1.

8. Wendy Erlich, "Can Children's Television Programming Be Improved through Public Policy?" (M.A. thesis, Annenberg School of Communications, University of Pennsylvania, 1973), p. 22.

9. "Mothers Fighting Radio Bogies," Literary Digest, no. 115, March 18, 1933, p. 32; and "Radio Horror for Children Only," American Mercury 44 (July 1938): 294-301.

10. Anthony M. Maltese, "A Descriptive Study of Children's Programming on Major American Television Networks from 1950 through 1964" (Ph.D. diss., Ohio University, 1967), p. 12.

11. "Gun, Gat, and Rod," Time, March 3, 1952, p. 70; and "Two Year Study of Viewing Habits of Children," Newsweek, April 29, 1954, p. 91.

12. Quoted in Gilberg Seldes, "Under the Eyes of Eternity," Saturday Review of Literature, August 14, 1954, p. 25.

13. Erik Barnouw, The Image Empire (New York: Oxford University Press, 1970), p. 83; and Maltese, "Children's Programming," p. 8.

14. National Association of Broadcasters, The Television Code, Effective March 1, 1952 (Washington, D. C.: National Association of Broadcasters, 1952), p. 3.

15. Ibid.

16. Maltese, "Children's Programming," p. 145.

17. Melody, Children's Television, pp. 44-46.

18. Barnouw, The Image Empire, p. 83.

19. National Association of Broadcasters, Television Code, July 1956 (Washington, D. C.: National Association of Broadcasters, 1956), p. 3.

20. Ibid.

21. Barry Litman, "The Television Networks, Competition, and Program Diversity," Journal of Broadcasting 23 (Fall 1979): 403.

22. Maltese, "Children's Programming," p. 145.

23. Ibid., p. 62.

24. Melody, Children's Television, p. 19.

25. Interview with William Weiss, Terrytoon executive.

# 3
## SHAPING A PROGRAMMING FORM, 1960-69

Many of the approaches to children's program diversity followed by ABC, CBS, and NBC in the late 1950s continued past the turn of the decade. Throughout the 1960s, however, the pattern of diversity became so clear—and so narrow—that the scheduling and makeup of juvenile series became much more easily predictable than before.

### THE ECONOMIC AND SOCIAL ENVIRONMENT

The early and late 1960s vibrated with political and social activism aimed at producers of children's television, while the middle years passed in relative calm. The decade began with a double-barreled attack on the networks from two government bodies—the Senate and the Federal Communications Commission (FCC). The senator making waves in 1961 was Thomas Dodd who, as chairman of the Subcommittee on Juvenile Delinquency, took up Estes Kefauver's gauntlet and focused on television violence. Coming in the wake of the national attention and congressional investigation aimed at cheating on television's adult quiz programs in 1959, the television violence hearings bestowed upon beleaguered network officials further embarrassing visibility. Dodd did not focus specifically on children's television. Nevertheless, he made broadcasting executives nervous about all their programming as his exposure of industry practices encouraging television violence won "banner headlines and letters from aroused parents, educators, clergy, police, psychiatrists, and social workers."[1]

By 1962, however, Dodd's hearings looked a lot less threatening to broadcasters. The hearings had seen network supporters respond to criticisms of violence in action-adventure fare by emphasizing the lack of proof that television violence caused juvenile delinquency and crime. Having developed a perspective they would voice repeatedly throughout the decade, network supporters forcefully held to the conviction that no causal link existed between television and crime and that television violence did not shape, but rather mirrored, a violent society.[2] Moreover, broadcasters began to realize that the senator was more concerned with winning campaign contributors and friends among their industry's elite than with pushing his case against television violence. Dodd's subcommittee never did make its report public. Network officials were not, however, nearly so sanguine about rumblings from the FCC chairman, Newton Minow. Minow, appointed in 1960 by President Kennedy, was honest, articulate, and not hesitant to remind broadcasters that there was "nothing permanent or sacred about a broadcast license."[3] He was committed to spurring television licensees on to airing better programming, especially better programming for children. He made that point in a 1961 address to the National Association of Broadcasters.

> It used to be said that there were three great influences
> on a child: home, school and church. Today, there is a
> fourth great influence, and you ladies and gentlemen con-
> trol it. . . . What about your responsibilities? Is there
> no room in television to teach, to inform, to uplift, to
> stretch, to enlarge the capacities of our children? Is
> there no room for reading the great literature of the past,
> teaching them the great traditions of freedom?[4]

It was clear to industry watchers that several of the nonfiction children's series of the early 1960s ("Discovery," "One, Two Three—Go!" "Exploring," and "Reading Room") were direct responses to pressures exerted by Minow and, to a lesser degree, by Dodd. Network personnel admitted that ideas for such programs had incubated at the networks for some time but that executives would not allow their production until Minow's arrival.[5] After Minow left the FCC in 1963 (a few months before President Kennedy's assassination), many in the television industry felt the pressure to televise "prestige" children's programming had diminished considerably. The new chairman, E. William Henry, was not expected to be as tough.[6]

The years 1963 through 1967 saw a decided downturn in the level of debate regarding children's television. Governmental agencies and public pressure groups moved on to other subjects. One organization that continued to raise the children's television issue was the National Association for Better Radio and Television (NAFBRAT), which had been tilling the soil of broadcast advocacy for over 15 years. In 1965 NAFBRAT released its first "comprehensive guide for family viewing," an annotated listing of 344 network and syndicated television series meant to guide parents in regulating the viewing behavior of children. The guide bemoaned the "lack of sufficient programs of value for children" and added that "many of the programs that are aired for children, or during hours when children constitute a large proportion of the audience, are full of death, brutality, and terror devices which are almost universally deplored by authorities in the fields of education, law enforcement, religion, and mental health."[7] Seven of the 27 network children's series listed by the guide were described as fully objectionable for child viewing, mainly because of excessive violence. Although NAFBRAT's evaluation committee did not deal explicitly with the issue of diversity, it did note a need for "programs which provide wholesome humor, creative entertainment, social values, and use of the imagination."[8]

NAFBRAT released a "family viewing guide" annually from 1965 through the 1970s. While having a fairly wide distribution, it never became the center of controversy, nor did it seem to influence network programming policy. NAFBRAT Guide Editor Frank Orme admitted as much in 1968 when he declared that the season's children's fare was "the worst yet . . . a mass of indiscriminate entertainment dominated by some 40 animated program series which are, in turn, dominated by ugliness, noise, and violence."[9] Actually, NAFBRAT was only indirectly an activist organization. It termed its guide educational and hoped that enlightened audiences would eventually bring network programmers to schedule more enlightened fare. In any event, neither NAFBRAT nor other groups hoping to encourage change in children's television had the easy visibility of a federal forum in the mid-1960s. The government had turned to other matters, and children's television was not a priority.

As it turned out, the year NAFBRAT termed the worst ever was also the year a number of circumstances coalesced to again bring the subject of children's television to the attention of the public. The assassinations of Martin Luther King and Robert Kennedy shocked many leaders into a reconsideration of violence in U.S. life. Riots at the Democratic National Convention in Chicago added to the horror. Inevitably, the subject of television's contribution to U.S. violence was raised, both within television's creative community and outside.[10] The National Commission on the Causes and Prevention of Violence, headed by Milton Eisenhower, was convened to study the general problem of violence and decided to investigate television as a possible factor. In 1969 the task force report condemned "serious, non-comic" violent elements in children's shows.[11] Also in 1969 Senator John Pastore, chairman of the House Subcommittee on Communications, asked the U.S. surgeon general to commission a study of televised violence and its effect on viewers. Children were to be a particular focus of the wide-ranging series of investigations.

It was in 1969 that Action for Children's Television (ACT) first entered the national scene as an activist organization interested in changing children's television. The organization had been founded a year earlier but had not ventured beyond the Boston area. In October 1969 Evelyn Sarson, president of ACT, wrote a letter to the New York Times emphasizing that commercialism, not violence, was the greatest evil in children's television and arguing the need for age-specific programming. Around the same time, Lillian Ambrosino represented ACT before Senator Pastore's communications subcommittee, which was considering the FCC appointments of Dean Burch and Robert Wells. ACT did not oppose their appointments but asked "what they think the FCC can and should do" about rampant commercialism in children's television and the unmet "special needs" of children for age-specific programming. [12]

Not until a new decade had begun (January 1970) did the members of ACT meet with network officials for the first time. [13] According to Historian Barnouw, the social traumas of 1967, some coming after ABC, NBC, and CBS had decided on their 1969 television schedules, did cause the networks to alter their children's schedules slightly for the last year of the decade. "Networks scrapped some of the violent cartoons still crowding Saturday morning schedules. NBC installed a live animal series and a children's quiz." [14] During a large part of the 1960s, however, the television networks apparently felt relatively secure from the influence of governmental bodies and public pressure groups on programming. "The biggest crisis faced by the TV networks," said CBS television vice-president and programming chief Michael Dann in 1966, "is the fact that we're running out of movies." [15]

While societal pressures waxed hot and cold, industry pressures operated to shape the economic environment surrounding programmers throughout the decade. By the early 1960s, the networks had begun to realize that some advertisers (particularly snack companies and toy companies) were interested in reaching only children and that the networks' emphasis on "family programming" was driving those advertisers to sponsor juvenile programs through the local stations rather than pay for both adults and children on network television. The networks had released the late afternoon "children's hour" to their affiliates and now found themselves losing advertisers because of it. Their competitive move was to replace their lost afternoon slot with the underutilized Saturday morning and to offer rate discounts with the hope of attracting advertisers to that period. In addition, ABC, CBS, and NBC encouraged advertisers that did not want to sponsor a program alone to share sponsorship with others or "purchase" participating" time on programs the networks had licensed from production companies and scheduled themselves. [16] Sponsors of children's series were increasingly attracted to shared and participating sponsorship throughout the decade. By its end, each form of joint support was more common than full support by one firm, for economic reasons. Growth of color broadcasting during the 1960s made some of the old theatricals used in the 1950s obsolete, and creating new program material was very expensive. As Melody points out, new material "had to be broadcast several times over an extended period to amortize expenses, a tremendous risk for a single sponsor."[17] Consequently, sharing expenses with one or two other companies was preferable to sole sponsorship for some advertisers. Even more desirable for others was participation, since with that arrangement the network bore the risk of series creation, and the advertiser simply bought time during a particular episode. Another attraction of participation was its freeing of advertisers from placing all their commercial bets on one program; it allowed them to scatter their commercials throughout the schedule (and on more than one network), thus reaching many different children as possible.

The networks, for their part, encouraged the move to participation because it gave them control over series development, and often over profits from series successes. In addition, participation allowed the networks more discretion than ever before regarding program lineups and, by extension, programming strategies.[18] Here the networks were applying lessons they learned in prime time. In the early 1960s network programmers developed scheduling strategies designed to keep family and adult audiences with their affiliates during the entire period from 7:00 P.M. to 11:00 P.M. The possibility of copying these techniques to attract children to a network for several hours at a time may have further encouraged programmers to use a circumscribed period—Saturday morning—for scheduling children's fare. In addition to supporting these new sponsorship and scheduling tendencies, network executives had to have realized that a sponsor's ultimate measure of a juvenile program's advertising value was its ability to reach a mass of youngsters at a lower cost than could be achieved through other television fare. Consequently, network programmers' essential criterion for series selection in the 1960s was the same as that used in the earlier decade. A series was desirable if it could attract youngsters to the shows' commercials on a cost-efficient basis.

THE RANGE OF PROGRAMMING

The following pages will, in large part, explore the consequences of this economic criterion for diversity in children's programming during the 1960s. It is true that active public pressures specifically voicing demands for more variation in programming tugged fiercely at the networks in the early part of the decade (until Minow's departure) and at its end (through the demands of ACT). However, during several middle years (from around 1964 through 1968), a kind of laissez-faire period reigned in children's television, and network programmers had a chance to follow the economic criterion relatively unencumbered. The consequences were quite visible in every area of program content from middecade and beyond. Emerging trends in scheduling, subject matter, format, and characterization that had been somewhat obscured in the late 1950s suddenly became apparent. Often, though not always, diversity suffered as a result. By decade's end, a quite consistent—and relatively homogeneous—shape to children's television could be discerned.

Scheduling and Program Duration

In terms of scheduling and program duration, developments of the late 1950s solidified as trends in the 1960s. The drop from 41 series in 1956-57 to 28 series in 1958-59 was followed by a continuation of this relatively small number of series in the next four two-year periods. Table 3.1 shows that it was not until 1968-69 that the number of programs for children even matched the number telecast during any two-year span from 1952-53 through 1956-57. With a few exceptions, each of the networks held to this pattern. More generally, the drop in shows also reflected a drop in weekly hours taken up by children's fare. Table 3.2 indicates that the decrease in weekly hours was much more drastic than the drop in series. Moreover, it shows that, even by the end of the decade, there were fewer weekly hours devoted to children's series than at any time from 1951 to 1956 (see Table 2.2). Another difference between the number of shows and the number of hours related to the individual networks. While all three networks took turns carrying the largest number of programs during the 1960s, CBS consistently programmed the largest number of weekly hours. CBS aired a minimum of 9.5 hours (in 1960-61) and a maximum of 19 hours (in 1968-69). By contrast, NBC's hours ranged from a low of five in 1964-65 and 1966-67 to a high of 7.5 in 1968-69, and ABC's hours ranged from a low of 3.5 hours in 1962-63 to a high of 7.5 hours in 1968-69.

These trends in children's programming throughout the 1960s echo earlier discussions of industry and nonindustry influences on the networks and sponsors. The number of programs decreased in the late 1950s because sponsors deserted the "children's hour" for family programming in prime time, and the networks began to give up the late afternoon slot to their affiliates. In the early 1960s the number increased slowly, as network officials became aware that some ad-

TABLE 3.1

Distribution of Children's Series by Networks, 1960-69
(in percent)

|  | 1960–61 (N = 31) | 1962–63 (N = 29) | 1964–65 (N = 34) | 1966–67 (N = 37) | 1968–69 (N = 49) |
|---|---|---|---|---|---|
| ABC | 39 | 28 | 38 | 32 | 30 |
| CBS | 26 | 31 | 32 | 38 | 43 |
| NBC | 35 | 41 | 29 | 30 | 27 |
| Total | 100 | 100 | 99 | 100 | 100 |

Note: Totals less than 100 percent are due to rounding error.

Source: Compiled by the author.

vertisers wanted to reach only children and as they began to develop their marketplace anew. An important stage of readjustment and re-location of children's programming was completed by decade's end.

Part of that readjustment involved the increased standardiza-tion of the length of children's series to a half hour. The movement toward the half hour as the common length for children's series began in the mid-1950s. Recall from Chapter 2 that in the late 1940s and early 1950s around 60 percent of the series lasted 30 minutes, with

TABLE 3.2

Weekly Hours Taken Up by Children's Series, 1960-69
(in percent)

|  | 1960–61 | 1962–63 | 1964–65 | 1966–67 | 1968–69 |
|---|---|---|---|---|---|
| ABC | 6.00 | 3.50 | 6.00 | 5.50 | 7.50 |
| CBS | 9.50 | 9.50 | 10.50 | 12.00 | 19.00 |
| NBC | 7.00 | 7.16 | 5.00 | 5.00 | 7.50 |
| Total | 22.50 | 20.16 | 21.50 | 22.50 | 34.00 |

Note: The table does not include series scheduled less than once a week.

Source: Compiled by the author.

TABLE 3.3

Weekly Frequency of Children's Programs, 1960-69
(in percent)

|  | 1960-61 (N = 31) | 1962-63 (N = 29) | 1964-65 (N = 34) | 1966-67 (N = 37) | 1968-69 (N = 49) |
|---|---|---|---|---|---|
| Less than once | 7 | 3 | 3 | 2 | 2 |
| Once | 87 | 90 | 94 | 95 | 96 |
| Twice | 3 | 0 | 0 | 0 | 0 |
| Three times | 0 | 0 | 0 | 0 | 0 |
| Four times | 0 | 0 | 0 | 0 | 0 |
| Five times | 0 | 3 | 0 | 0 | 0 |
| Six times | 3 | 3 | 3 | 3 | 2 |
| Seven times | 0 | 0 | 0 | 0 | 0 |
| Total | 100 | 99 | 100 | 100 | 100 |
| Diversity index | .764 | .813 | .885 | .904 | .922 |

Note: Totals less than 100 percent are due to rounding error.

Source: Compiled by the author.

the rest lasting 15 minutes or, less likely, an hour. By the end of
the 1950s, however, half-hour shows had climbed gradually to between
80 percent and 90 percent of the total. The 1960s established this
level as the norm. In fact, 1960-61 and 1966-67 exceeded that level.
During those years, 30-minute programs comprised 94 percent and
95 percent of the series, respectively. In the 1960s, 15-minute
series totally disappeared. Hour-long programs fluctuated between
5 percent and 15 percent of the whole. Interestingly, one unusual
time frame did intrude upon the extremely low diversity of program
duration in that decade. During 1961-62 "Burr Tillstrom's Kukla,
Fran, and Ollie" aired for five minutes on Mondays through Fridays
at 5:00 P.M.
　　Accompanying the standardization of program duration was a
standardization of the number of times a series aired in a week. Once-
a-week programming characterized 52 percent of the series in 1950-
51, 70 percent in 1954-55, and 76 percent in 1958-59. It became even
more dominant in the 1960s. Table 3.3 indicates that once-a-week
series increased from 87 percent and 90 percent of the total in 1960-61

and 1962-63, to 95 percent and 96 percent of the total in 1966-67 and 1968-69, respectively. Comparing the table's diversity index with that of Table 2.4 indicates that there was much less diversity in program frequency in the 1960s than the 1950s. Whereas the index read .594 in 1958-59, it read .922 in 1968-69. (The highest possible number is 1.0.) Totally nonexistent during the 1960s were programs telecast three or four times a week. Only one program was telecast twice a week ("Pip the Piper" in 1960-61), and only one program aired five times a week ("Burr Tillstrom's Kukla, Fran, and Ollie" in 1962-63). "On Your Mark," short-lived as a network series during 1960-61, was designated, with "Young People's Concerts," as a program seen less than once a week during 1960-61. However, during the rest of the decade, only the prestige music series fit the category of less than once a week. Similarly, "Captain Kangaroo" was the only series telecast six times a week (Monday through Saturday) during the 1960s.

The standardization of children's series to a once-a-week, 30-minute schedule helps explain why the amount of weekly time devoted to programming in the early 1950s surpassed that devoted to programming in 1968-69, even though the number of series seen at least once a week was almost the same for both periods. The reason relates to the fairly high number of programs telecast more than once a week during 1950-51 and 1952-53 (21 and 12, respectively), compared with the very small number airing more than once a week in 1968-69 (1). In the 1950s the multiple telecasts were sometimes 15-minute shows, sometimes 30-minute programs. The substantial time they occupied when airing three, four, or five times a week helped bring the average weekly length of a program to 61 minutes in 1950-51 and 54 minutes in 1952-53. The average weekly duration of a program in 1966-67, by contrast, was only 43 minutes. Incidently, the fact that CBS's hour-long "Captain Kangaroo" remained the only program telecast more than once a week throughout the decade helps explain why that network consistently televised by far the largest number of weekly children's hours in the 1960s, even though it did not always air the largest number of programs.

As could be predicted from earlier discussion, a large part of the once-a-week programming was funneled into Saturday morning. Table 3.4 reflects a continuation of trends already emerging in Table 2.3. A comparison of the two tables shows the progressive reliance by the networks on Saturday morning as the anchor of children's series programming. In 1954-55, 20 percent of the children's shows were scheduled on Saturday morning. By 1958-59 that proportion had risen to 39 percent, and, in 1960-61, 51 percent of the children's series nestled in Saturday morning. A slight drop to 48 percent in 1962-63 was followed by a rise to 65 percent and 69 percent, respectively, in 1966-67 and 1968-69. Actually, Saturday morning took on

TABLE 3.4

Scheduling of Children's Programs, 1960-69
(in percent)

| | 1960-61 (N = 31) | 1962-63 (N = 29) | 1964-65 (N = 34) | 1966-67 (N = 37) | 1968-69 (N = 49) |
|---|---|---|---|---|---|
| Monday-Friday | | | | | |
| Morning (7:00-11:30) | 0 | 0 | 0 | 0 | 0 |
| Afternoon (12:00-4:00) | 0 | 0 | 0 | 0 | 0 |
| Early evening (4:30-7:00) | 0 | 3 | 0 | 0 | 0 |
| Prime time (7:00 P.M.-11:00 P.M.) | 0 | 0 | 0 | 0 | 0 |
| Friday alone | | | | | |
| Morning | 0 | 0 | 0 | 0 | 0 |
| Afternoon | 0 | 0 | 0 | 0 | 0 |
| Early evening | 0 | 0 | 0 | 0 | 0 |
| Prime time | 3 | 0 | 0 | 0 | 0 |
| One weekday (not Friday) | | | | | |
| Morning | 0 | 0 | 0 | 0 | 0 |
| Afternoon | 0 | 0 | 0 | 0 | 0 |
| Early evening | 3 | 0 | 0 | 0 | 0 |
| Prime time | 10 | 6 | 0 | 0 | 0 |
| Two to four weekdays | | | | | |
| Morning | 0 | 0 | 0 | 0 | 0 |
| Afternoon | 0 | 0 | 0 | 0 | 0 |
| Early evening | 3 | 0 | 0 | 0 | 0 |
| Prime time | 0 | 0 | 0 | 0 | 0 |
| Saturday | | | | | |
| Morning | 51 | 48 | 55 | 65 | 69 |
| Afternoon | 10 | 21 | 24 | 16 | 14 |
| Early evening | 0 | 0 | 0 | 0 | 0 |
| Prime time | 0 | 0 | 0 | 0 | 0 |
| Sunday | | | | | |
| Morning | 3 | 7 | 6 | 8 | 10 |
| Afternoon | 0 | 0 | 12 | 5 | 4 |
| Early evening | 10 | 7 | 0 | 3 | 0 |
| Prime time | 0 | 0 | 0 | 0 | 0 |
| One weekday and Saturday | | | | | |
| Morning/morning | 0 | 0 | 0 | 0 | 0 |
| Evening/morning | 0 | 0 | 0 | 0 | 0 |
| Other time combination | 0 | 0 | 0 | 0 | 0 |
| One weekday and Sunday | | | | | |
| Morning/morning | 0 | 0 | 0 | 0 | 0 |
| Evening/morning | 0 | 0 | 0 | 0 | 0 |
| Other time combination | 0 | 0 | 0 | 0 | 0 |
| Multiple weekday and Saturday | | | | | |
| Morning/morning | 3 | 3 | 3 | 3 | 2 |
| Evening/morning | 0 | 3 | 0 | 0 | 0 |
| Other time combination | 0 | 0 | 0 | 0 | 0 |
| Multiple weekday and Sunday | | | | | |
| Morning/morning | 0 | 0 | 0 | 0 | 0 |
| Evening/morning | 0 | 0 | 0 | 0 | 0 |
| Other time combination | 0 | 0 | 0 | 0 | 0 |
| Saturday and Sunday | | | | | |
| Morning/morning | 3 | 0 | 0 | 0 | 0 |
| Evening/morning | 0 | 0 | 0 | 0 | 0 |
| Other time combination | 0 | 0 | 0 | 0 | 0 |
| Total | 99 | 98 | 100 | 100 | 99 |
| Diversity index | .296 | .291 | .379 | .459 | .508 |

Note: Totals greater or less than 100 percent are due to rounding errors.

Source: Compiled by the author.

even greater importance than these numbers suggest, since it influenced the growth of the adjacent time period. The mid-1950s had seen a peak of 11 percent of children's programs on Saturday afternoon, but programs in that period declined to 7 percent and then 0 percent in the two-year spans that ended the decade. Beginning in 1960-61, however, Saturday afternoon programming rose again. It comprised 10 percent of the shows during that two-year span, 21 percent in 1962-63, and 24 percent in 1964-65, before it declined to 16 percent and 14 percent at decade's end. Despite the decline, the combined percentage of programs telecast on Saturday morning and afternoon rose steadily, from 61 percent in 1960-61 to 69 percent, 79 percent, 81 percent, and 83 percent throughout the decade.

The increased dominance of Saturday morning and afternoon programming naturally meant a decrease in the proportion of programs in other time slots. As a comparison of the diversity indexes in Tables 3.4 and 2.3 indicate, the use of various time slots to schedule children's series decreased strongly across the 1950s and 1960s. From a low of .089 in 1954-55, the diversity index rose to .182 in 1958-59, then rose again sharply in the next decade—to .296 in 1960-61, .379 in 1964-65, and .508 in 1968-69. Weekdays were the most common victims of this drop in scheduling diversity. "Captain Kangaroo" continued its Monday through Saturday airing throughout the decade. Monday through Friday programming ceased to exist in the 1960s (except for "Burr Tillstrom's Kukla, Fran, and Ollie" in 1962-63). Series found on two, three, or four weekdays disappeared after 1960-61. (During that two-year span, ABC switched "My Friend Flicka" around various weekly spots.) Aside from these programs, the only series not aired on weekends only was "Discovery." During most of 1963, that program aired on Saturday morning. However, in the early part of its run, the prestigious nonfiction show appeared as a 25-minute presentation in the afternoon on Monday through Friday. Later in "Discovery"'s first season, ABC scheduled highlights of the Saturday show at 10:30 P.M. on Tuesdays in order to publicize the program to adults. Because of these switches, the program is listed under "multiple weekday and Saturday" in the table.

While weekday programming experienced a precipitous drop in the 1960s, there was a more moderate decline in Sunday programming. Sunday in 1956-57 accounted for 35 percent of the network children's series, and Sunday in the next decade, between 12 percent and 19 percent of the series. More significant than these drops in percentages, however, was the elimination of children's series from many of the Sunday time periods. During most of the 1950s, children's shows were scheduled during Sunday morning, afternoon, early afternoon, and prime time. In the 1960s children's series were eliminated from prime time and were aired much less consistently in the early evening.

In fact, in 1968-69 Sunday morning and afternoon were virtually the only areas on the schedule other than Saturday to include a block of children's series.

The growth of Saturday morning as the primary "children's block" during the 1960s and the spillover of children's programming into Saturday afternoon are reflected in Figure 3.1. The figure records the material telecast by the ABC-, CBS-, and NBC-owned-and-operated stations in New York City on particular Saturdays in 1960 and 1969. The differences suggest the evolution of a coherent flow of network children's fare between the start and end of the decade. Saturday morning in 1960 was not unlike the Saturday morning examined in 1959. A total of five hours of network children's series was telecast, often connected by nonnetwork shows probably created for juveniles. However, several of the Saturday morning programs ("The Big Picture," "Modern Farmer," "Susie," "The Great Gildersleeve," and "I Love Lucy") were clearly not created for children. By contrast, 1969 saw a total of ten hours of network children's programs, most of them flowing continuously from 9:00 A.M. onward. Moreover, of the five nonnetwork programs aired before 9:00 A.M., only one ("Black Heritage") did not clearly have the mark of a show produced specifically for children.

The success of the 1969 children's block can be inferred from the networks' use of the time adjacent to Saturday morning for children's fare. CBS, in fact, continued its network children's schedule to 1:30 P.M., while ABC turned its attention to the teenage market with "American Bandstand." The NBC affiliate chose to follow ABC's example, using a nature program ("Untamed World") to bridge the gap between its network children's schedule and a quiz show ("It's Academic") for teenagers. An earlier, though much less consistent, version of this strategy could be seen in January 1960. At that time, only ABC ("Lunch with Soupy Sales") and CBS ("Sky King") continued children's programming past noon. The NBC station turned to reruns of programs created for adults ("True Story" and "Detective Diary"). At 12:30 P.M. the CBS station seemed to switch to a teenage orientation with the show "Young World," and the ABC affiliate (after showing the adult series "Restless Gun") turned to local high school basketball.

Subject Matter

Subject matter and format changes accompanied the funneling of network children's programs into a "block" on Saturday morning during the 1960s. Those changes took place less smoothly than did the scheduling changes. In fact, the mid-1960s formed a kind of

FIGURE 3.1

Saturday Morning and Afternoon Television, January 1960 and January 1969

January 16, 1960

Saturday Morning

7:00  No programs aired (ABC)
      The Big Picture (CBS) to 7:30
      Modern Farmer (CBS) to 8:00
7:30  No programs aired (ABC)
      Susie (CBS) to 8:00

8:00  Cartoons (ABC) to 11:00
      Captain Kangaroo (CBS) to 9:00
      Andy's Gang (NBC) to 8:30
8:30  Children's Theater (NBC) to 9:30

9:00  Captain Jet (NBC) to 10:00

9:30  Roy Rogers (NBC) to 10:00

10:00  Heckle and Jeckle (CBS) to 10:30
       Howdy Doody (NBC) to 10:30

10:30  Mighty Mouse (CBS) to 11:00
       Ruff and Ready (NBC) to 11:00

11:00  Great Gildersleeve (ABC) to 11:30
       I Love Lucy (CBS) to 11:30
       Fury (NBC) to 11:30
11:30  Magic Eye (ABC) to 12:00
       The Lone Ranger (CBS) to 12:00
       Circus Boy (NBC) to 12:00

Saturday Afternoon

12:00  Lunch with Soupy Sales (ABC) to 12:30
       Sky King (CBS) to 12:30
       True Story (NBC) to 12:30
12:30  Restless Gun (ABC) to 1:00
       Young World (CBS) to 1:00
       Detective's Diary (NBC) to 1:00
1:00   News (CBS) to 1:30
       Film (NBC) to 2:30
       High School Basketball (ABC) to 3:00
1:30   Eye on New York (CBS) to 2:00

2:00   Hockey (CBS) to 4:30

2:30   Bar 4 Films (NBC) to 4:00
3:00   Baseball (ABC) to 5:00

4:00   Sir Anthony Eden Interview (NBC) to
       4:30

January 11, 1969

Saturday Morning

7:00  No programs aired (ABC)
      No programs aired (CBS)
      No programs aired (NBC)
7:30  Davey and Goliath (ABC) to 8:00
      Black Heritage (CBS) to 8:00
      Colonel Bleep (NBC) to 8:30
8:00  Cartoons (ABC) to 9:00
      Go Go Gophers (CBS) to 8:30

8:30  Bugs Bunny/Road Runner (CBS) to 9:30
      Dodo (NBC) to 9:00
9:00  Casper Cartoons (ABC) to 9:30
      Super Six (NBC) to 9:30
9:30  Adventures of Gulliver (ABC) to 10:00
      Wacky Races (CBS) to 10:00
      Top Cat (NBC) to 10:00
10:00  Spiderman (ABC) to 10:30
       Archie Show (CBS) to 10:30
       Flintstones (NBC) to 10:30
10:30  Fantastic Voyage (ABC) to 11:00
       Batman/Superman (CBS) to 11:30
       Banana Splits (NBC) to 11:30
11:00  Journey to the Center of the Earth
       (ABC) to 11:30

11:30  Fantastic Four (ABC) to 12:00
       Herculoids (CBS) to 12:00
       Underdog (NBC) to 12:00

Saturday Afternoon

12:00  George of the Jungle (ABC) to 12:30
       Shazzan! (CBS) to 12:30
       Storybook Squares (NBC) to 12:30
12:30  American Bandstand (ABC) to 1:30
       Jonny Quest (CBS) to 1:00
       Untamed World (NBC) to 12:30
1:00   Moby Dick (CBS) to 2:00
       It's Academic (NBC) to 1:30

1:30   Happening (ABC) to 2:00
       Research Project (CBS) to 2:00
2:00   Movie (ABC) to 3:00
       Opportunity Line (CBS) to 2:30
       College Football (NBC) to 4:30
2:30   The Learning Experience (CBS) to 3:00
3:00   Celebrity Billiards (ABC) to 3:30
       Young World 69 (CBS) to 3:30
3:30   Pro Bowler's Tour (ABC) to 5:00
       Callback (CBS) to 4:00
4:00   Golf Classic (CBS) to 5:00

Note: The underscored programs are network children's series. New York time is used.
Source: New York Times.

62

watershed that led from a gradual transition to new program emphases into abrupt shifts to the new forms. This section and the next will investigate these changes and their consequences for subject and format diversity. In doing so, the discussion will most often center on network children's series in general. Of course, important differences between the Saturday morning "children's block" and the rest of network fare will be discussed. In general, though, trends in programming as a whole quite accurately reflected trends on Saturday morning. If there was any difference, it was that the Saturday morning series utilized only the most common subjects and format categories; that is, the networks did not use Saturday morning to inject unusual fare into the schedule.

Actually, a look at changes in main subjects between the late 1950s and the first half of the 1960s discovers few differences or unusual patterns. Tables 2.5 and 3.5 reveal a generally moderate fluctuation in the use of fiction, nonfiction, and performing activities across those years. Moreover, the distribution of all 24 subjects in the tables shows but a moderate decline in the diversity index from the late 1950s to the mid-1960s. This moderate decline reflects a slight widening of choice among performing activities and a somewhat larger percentage of programs devoted to nonfiction. Most of that nonfiction emphasized "a mixture of nonfiction"; the rest covered "other physical science." Performing categories also emphasized the general ("various performances"), but more specific topics were included as well ("competitive games," "music," and "magic"). In the fiction area, small changes tended to offset each other. The few storybook programs of the late 1950s were discontinued during the first half of the 1960s, but science fiction and a jungle-based adventure aired for the first time in a decade. Westerns and "other adventure" tended to decline in prominence, while series using unrelated fiction segments tended to increase.

The late 1960s saw much more dramatic changes. Series mixing fiction, nonfiction, and performing activities continued to hold steady at about 3 percent throughout the decade. However, programs exclusively involving performing activities fell sharply—from 27 percent and 18 percent of the total in 1962-63 and 1964-65 to 3 percent in 1966-67 and 4 percent at decade's end. Nonfiction experienced a similar drop, from 20 percent in 1962-63 to 8 percent in 1966-67 and 4 percent at decade's end. In turn, fiction programming became overwhelmingly dominant after middecade. From 61 percent, 47 percent, and 66 percent of programming in the early two-year spans of the 1960s, fiction series soared in 1966-67 and 1968-69 to 87 percent and 92 percent of the whole. The change was even more dramatic on Saturday morning alone. After characterizing 56 percent of the Saturday morning series in 1962-63, fiction rose to 80 percent in 1964-65 and to 100 percent in 1966-67 and 1968-69.

TABLE 3.5

Main Subjects of Children's Series, 1960–69
(in percent)

| | 1960–61 (N = 31) | 1962–63 (N = 29) | 1964–65 (N = 34) | 1966–67 (N = 37) | 1968–69 (N = 49) |
|---|---|---|---|---|---|
| Fiction | | | | | |
| Storybook | 7 | 3 | 0 | 0 | 0 |
| Western | 16 | 14 | 15 | 3 | 4 |
| Police | 0 | 0 | 0 | 14 | 27 |
| Science fiction | 0 | 0 | 9 | 11 | 4 |
| Jungle or "wilds" | 3 | 3 | 3 | 5 | 8 |
| Other adventure | 10 | 3 | 8 | 22 | 27 |
| Adventure in different settings | 0 | 0 | 3 | 0 | 0 |
| Realistic problem drama | 0 | 0 | 0 | 0 | 0 |
| Unrelated dramatic sequences | 25 | 24 | 28 | 32 | 22 |
| Nonfiction | | | | | |
| ABCs, arithmetic | 0 | 0 | 0 | 0 | 0 |
| History | 0 | 0 | 0 | 0 | 0 |
| Geography | 0 | 0 | 0 | 0 | 0 |
| Nature | 0 | 0 | 0 | 5 | 2 |
| Other physical science | 3 | 3 | 6 | 0 | 0 |
| Occupations | 0 | 0 | 0 | 0 | 0 |
| Biography | 0 | 0 | 0 | 0 | 0 |
| Religion | 0 | 0 | 0 | 0 | 0 |
| Mixture nonfiction | 10 | 17 | 9 | 3 | 2 |
| Performing activities | | | | | |
| Child sports | 0 | 0 | 0 | 0 | 0 |
| Competitive games | 3 | 3 | 6 | 0 | 2 |
| Magic | 0 | 7 | 3 | 0 | 0 |
| Music | 3 | 3 | 3 | 3 | 2 |
| Various performances | 16 | 14 | 6 | 0 | 0 |
| Subject mixture | 3 | 3 | 3 | 3 | 2 |
| Total | 99 | 97 | 102 | 101 | 102 |
| Diversity index | .143 | .137 | .117 | .191 | .205 |

Note: Totals greater or less than 100 percent are due to rounding error.

Source: Compiled by the author.

The sharp decrease in performing activities and nonfiction in the schedule as a whole, as well as on Saturday morning alone, helps explain the rise of the diversity index in 1966-67 and 1968-69 to levels exceeding those of all previous two-year spans but 1948-49. That the index was not even higher at the end of the 1960s is attributable to the spread of fiction across more categories than before. Some specific changes in fiction programming from previous years are noteworthy. Of greatest significance were the continued decrease of the once-dominant fiction formula, the western, and the rise of both the police adventure and "other adventure" categories. Westerns decreased sharply, from 15 percent at middecade to 3 percent and 4 percent in 1966-67 and 1968-69, respectively. Around the same time, series dealing with police or various other agents of the law (who were not in western or science fiction plots) appeared for the first time since "Captain Midnight"—and comprised a strong 14 percent and 27 percent, respectively, of all the series. Series with unrelated fiction sequences also formed an important category, though it fluctuated from highs of 28 percent and 32 percent in 1964-65 and 1966-67, respectively, to 22 percent in 1968-69 (the same level it occupied in the late 1950s). Three categories were as inconsequential in the 1960s as they were in the 1950s: "adventures in different settings," "storybook" programs, and series dealing with everyday ("realistic") problems of children made no appearance at all in 1966-67 and 1968-69.

The number of programs that originated during the 1950s and still aired in the 1960s diminished as the decade progressed. In 1960-61, 45 percent of the series had been carried over from the previous decade. In 1962-63 the series from the previous decade comprised 24 percent of the total, and, in subsequent two-year spans, they comprised 18 percent, 8 percent, and 4 percent of the total. Interestingly, only one of the nonfiction series that aired during the 1950s ("Watch Mr. Wizard") made a transition to the next decade. Performing activities from the 1950s were only a bit more common at the start of the 1960s. In 1960-61, of the seven programs using performing activities ("Howdy Doody," "Young People's Concerts," "Paul Winchell Show," "Lunch with Soupy Sales," "Magic Land of Allakazam," "On Your Mark," and "Video Village Junior"), only three had aired in the previous decade.

Clearly, most of the series crossing from 1958-59 to 1960-61 were fiction. Several of these were westerns. In fact, the fairly strong presence of westerns in comparison with other categories at the start of the decade is attributable to such returnees as "The Lone Ranger," "Adventures of Rin Tin Tin," "Fury," and "Sky King." With the disappearance of these series during the decade, the children's western declined. Only two new westerns aired during the 1960s—"Annie Oakley" (1964-65) and the comedic "Go Go Gophers" (1968-69).

The western was the most extreme case of the existence of a fiction category depending upon series from the previous decade. Other categories mixed the old with the new, and some relied only on the new. "Series with unrelated fiction segments" was a category that leaned both on the past and the present in the early 1960s. For example, "Mighty Mouse Playhouse" and "The Heckle and Jeckle Show" continued to air during 1960-61, when "Rocky and His Friends," "Bullwinkle," "Bugs Bunny," and "King Leonardo" made their debuts. Only one series from the "other adventure" category ("Circus Boy") carried over from the 1950s, but other programs of that kind were introduced to children's television throughout the decade. Examples were "My Friend Flicka" (the adventures of a horse-raising family in the early 1900s), "The Flintstones" (the shenanigans of a prehistoric family patterned after Jackie Gleason's adult comedy "The Honeymooners"), "The Beatles" (the songs and fictional misadventures of the famous rock group), and "The Beagles" (the songs and misadventures of two dogs who form a rock duo).

Storybook shows and science fiction did not carry over from the 1950s at all. Only one storybook series was telecast during the 1960s, though it aired in different versions on two networks (ABC and NBC). The show was "Pip the Piper," a musical fantasy about a man named Pip who traveled on a private cloud each week to visit enchanted Pipertown. There were five science fiction programs, all beginning in the mid-1960s—"The Jetsons" (essentially "The Flintstones" in the future), "Fireball XL-5" (a futuristic police force), "Space Ghost" (the exploits of an intergalactic crime fighter with the power to make himself invisible), "Space Kiddettes" (a club of space-age youngsters fighting evil), and "The Herculoids" (mighty animals of a future era who protect their planet from evil invaders). ("The Jetsons" actually counts as three series in Table 3.5, since, at different times, it appeared on ABC, CBS, and NBC.)

It is interesting to note that at a time when civil unrest and anti-war protests were sweeping the nation, most of the science fiction programs emphasized the maintenance of law and order. Programs about other police or law agents accentuated this trend in the late 1960s. Just a list of some titles—"Superman," "Underdog," "Secret Squirrel," "Adventures of Aquaman," "Batman/Superman Hour"—implies the major elements shared by these series. Working off the time-tested "Superman" formula (and often showing the hero as meek in daily life), the series presented a world in dire danger that only a being with superhuman strength or cunning could confront and dispel. The hero did ally himself with established law agents of the society but quite often took his own initiative in seeking and solving the problem. While such heroes tended to populate series in the "other police and law agents" category, some could be found in series with unre-

lated fiction segments. Examples were "Mighty Mouse Playhouse,"
"Mighty Mouse and the Mighty Heroes," "Rocky and His Friends,"
and its variant "Bullwinkle." Deserving special mention because of
its fascinating method of wrapping a democratic aura around the traditionally individual superhero responsible to no elected body was a
series with a central segment entitled "Super President."

The science fiction, superhero, and law-and-order themes that
pervaded network children's programming in the late 1960s indicated
the pervasiveness of action-adventure—the controversial plot line
that had become increasingly common during much of the 1950s. Recall that "action-adventure" stories are tales in which protagonists
consistently (and often violently) pursue and battle evil in their envi-
ronments. Chapter 2 noted that series whose action-adventure plot
lines were central rose from 10 percent of the total in the late 1940s
to 37 percent in 1956-57, before dropping to 29 percent at decade's
end. That proportion dropped further in the early 1960s (the Minow
and Dodd years) to 26 percent in 1960-61, 10 percent in 1962-63, and
15 percent in 1964-65. In 1966-67, however, the tide turned sharply
toward action-adventure again. During that two-year span, 40 percent of all network children's series had the action-adventure stamp,
and, in 1968-69, the figure rose to 51 percent. Capsule descriptions
of series from the late 1960s will illustrate how programs with quite
different titles really ended up treading similar paths in only somewhat different garb.

"Birdman": An American, Ray Randall, receives amazing powers of flight and strength from the Egyptian Sun
God, Ra, and becomes the crime-fighting Birdman. His
battles against evil are aided by the Galaxy Trio—Vapor
Man, Galaxy Girl, and Meteor Man.

"Fantastic Four": Four Americans (three men and a
woman) acquire fantastic powers as the result of an ac-
cident during a space flight. One acquires the ability to
stretch around anything, another the ability to become
invisible at will, a third the strength of a Samson, and
the fourth the ability to become a human torch. The four
use these powers to combat evil.

"Samson and Goliath": A young boy, Samson, and his
dog, Goliath, battle crime and corruption in modern society. When in trouble, Samson raises his wrists,
touches his bracelets, and says, "I need Samson Power."
Thereupon he is transformed into a facsimile of the bibli-
cal Samson, and his dog is changed into a powerful lion.

"Space Ghost": Space Ghost is a crime fighter of the future, in the tradition of radio's "The Shadow." He receives his power of invisibility from a magic belt.

"Spider-Man": A young reporter for a New York newspaper has the web-spinning and climbing ability of the spider and uses it to battle criminals.

It should be noted that a large portion of the children's series that were not action-adventures nevertheless maintained an action-filled tempo through the "comic-chase" plot line. Many of the series with unrelated segments (for example, "Tom and Jerry," "Bugs Bunny," "Road Runner," and "Quick Draw McGraw") used the comic chase as a pivotal element. By the late 1960s, with the reduction of performing activities and nonfiction, the comic chase helped action-adventure fantasies virtually blanket network children's television with frenetic movement.

As the above descriptions of series implied, one feature that did distinguish some action-adventures from others was their placement in time. The emergence of science fiction during the mid- and late 1960s explains the use of "the future" as the time setting for a number of children's series for the first time since 1954-55. At the same time, the decline of the western from the late 1950s and early 1960s to the late 1960s explains, in large part, the decrease in programs dealing with the "historical past," from 13 percent of all series in 1960-61 and 18 percent in 1964-65 to 3 percent in 1966-67 and 6 percent in 1968-69. Clearly, "mixed" time periods appeared in 2 or 3 percent of the shows sporadically throughout the decade. The level of "mixed" time periods may be underestimated, however, since the rise of series containing unrelated fictional segments (including some that did not repeat every week) made it impossible to determine the time period of between 4 and 10 percent of all series throughout the decade.

Despite these changes, "the present" remained the time period in which the majority of series took place, whether they dealt with fiction, nonfiction, or performing activities. The proportion of programs set in the present never matched the high of 83 percent seen in 1956-57. However, it sometimes came close to that figure, fluctuating from 77 percent and 79 percent to 65 percent and 74 percent throughout the decade's two-year spans.

The maintenance of "the present" as the dominant time period came in spite of deviations by science fiction programs and series with unrelated fiction segments. At the same time, those programs, along with police and "other adventure" series, made fantasy the dominant orientation of children's programming. Fantasy's growth was initially quite gradual. Its upswing from 26 percent of the programs in 1956-57 to 34 percent in 1958-59 was followed by consistent increases to 39 percent, 41 percent, and 53 percent of the total from 1960-61 through 1964-65. Thus, in 1964-65, for the first time since the start of commercial network children's television, fantasy programs exceeded those based on reality. The true watershed period came in the next two-year span, however, when fully 84 percent of all children's series were fantasies. In the following two years, 86 percent of the shows were fantasies. At the same time, programs emphasizing "reality" went into decline. "Reality" series (for example, "My Friend Flicka," "Circus Boy," and "Discovery") dropped from 64 percent in 1956-57 to 55 percent in 1962-63, 41 percent in 1964-65, 14 percent in 1966-67, and 8 percent in 1968-69. Programs mixing reality and fantasy fluctuated between 3 percent and 10 percent during those years, never gaining the numerical prominence they had during some two-year spans in the 1950s.

The movement toward fantasy programming in the 1960s virtually snuffed out explicit attempts to motivate children toward understanding and participating in their surrounding world. The fact that no children's dramatic series dealt with realistic, everyday problems was nothing new; none had done so since the start of commercial television. And, as in the past, only one program could be said to have had a minority ethnic orientation. That the program was "Shazzan!" a series that used a genie as a device for yet another superhero, action-adventure tale, only served to reinforce the strong tendency toward uniformity in children's television by the late 1960s. What was new in the decade, however, was the strong and consistent decrease in the percentage of programs overtly trying to involve children at home. For the greater part of the 1950s, that figure hovered between 14 and 20 percent. In 1958-59, the figure had dropped to 10 percent, and, although it rose to 13 percent in 1960-61, it fell sharply throughout the rest of the decade—to 6 percent in 1962-63 and 1964-65, 3 percent in 1966-67, and 2 percent in 1968-69. These percentages represented five shows—"Captain Kangaroo" (in which the title character often spoke directly to his viewers), the two incarnations of "Pip the Piper" (in which, as part of the musical story, children were sometimes taught to make a costume or work at a craft), "Outside In" (a series that attempted to convince children of the joy of reading), and "Do You Know?" (a quiz program that solicited teams from elementary schools across the United States). After 1964-65, only "Captain Kangaroo" remained to explicitly attempt to involve children at home. A fairly logical outgrowth of children's programming when it first aired, the series was by then an anomaly in a children's television schedule that was dominated by action-filled adventure.

Significantly, the growth of fantasy in the Saturday morning block was even stronger than its growth in programming as a whole.

Actually, during much of the 1950s, fantasy exceeded reality on Saturday morning. In 1950-51, three of the five Saturday morning series emphasized reality, with the other two split between fantasy and "mixed." In 1952-53 reality shows dropped to 40 percent of the total, "mixed" rose to 40 percent, and fantasy remained at 20 percent. Beginning in 1954-55, however, fantasy rose above the other two orientations. It climbed to 42 percent of the Saturday total and then went a bit higher (to 44 percent) in 1954-55. "Mixed" comprised 22 percent and 17 percent, respectively, of the series during those years, and reality, 33 percent and 42 percent of the shows. The new decade brought a sharp decline for programs mixing reality and fantasy (to between 7 percent and 4 percent throughout the 1960s) and an increase in the presence of fantasy. As in programming as a whole, that rise was initially gradual. From 41 percent of the total in 1960-61, fantasy programs rose to 50 percent and 60 percent, respectively, in 1962-63 and 1964-65. The dramatic turn came in 1966-67 and 1968-69, when 92 percent, then 89 percent, of the programming bent toward fantasy. Programming based on reality, which rose briefly to 53 percent in 1960-61, fell to below 10 percent at decade's end.

The total immersion of the Saturday morning children's block in fantasy by the late 1960s points to the fact that Saturday morning programming accentuated the trend toward the use of main subjects—"other adventure," "science fiction," and "series with unrelated fiction segments"—that were seen dominating programming as a whole. Particularly worth mentioning is the general emphasis on action-adventure programming during the main children's slot of the late 1960s. For example, in 1966-67, 64 percent of the 25 Saturday morning series were action-adventures, and, in 1968-69, 74 percent of the 34 Saturday morning series fit that description. No nonfiction shows or programs with performing activities entered the Saturday morning children's block during those years. It is important to point out, however, that in 1968-69 the brunt of action-adventure programming came during the first year in the two-year span. The general consternation over the assassinations of Martin Luther King and Robert Kennedy forced the networks to tone down the violence on their 1969 children's schedules, and they removed many action-adventure series. Therefore, the January 1969 children's schedule reproduced in Figure 3.1 found action-adventures comprising only seven (41 percent) of the 17 Saturday morning network series.

Format

Throughout the 1960s, the increasing domination of children's programming by action-filled, fantasy series accompanied an increasing domination by animation. The reason was economic. During the 1950s the networks as well as the local stations had managed to keep their children's series cost-efficient (that is, had maintained a low cost of reaching youngsters for advertisers) by using inexpensive, studio-based formats (puppet shows and variety series) and by recycling old theatrical live-action or animated films. Melody notes that, by the end of the 1950s, "the old program supplies were dwindling," and broadcasters were looking for new sources for children's fare. [19] The need for new programming became particularly urgent in the mid-1960s as network programmers began to realize that eventually all their material would have to air in color. Old black-and white cowboy films would not do.

However, new animated material, produced in color, surely would. Animation was preferred over live action largely because a new technique for producing cartoons had dramatically reduced their costs. Generally speaking, until the 1950s, animated films of the kind the Disney organization made, or even of the type shown between live-action pictures in movie theaters, were expensive to produce. Hundreds of drawings were required for each scene. The time needed to complete projects was much too long for new products to be of major use for television series, which require many episodes within the space of a few months. [20] By the early 1950s, however, United Productions of America (UPA) introduced an alternative to this time-consuming process in its "Gerald McBoing Boing" theatrical shorts. [21] Called "limited animation," the technique involved moving the minimal elements of each frame that would keep up the action and tell the story. "The Boing Boing Show" televised the "Gerald McBoing Boing" theatricals over CBS from 1957 through 1958. But it was left to two former workers in Metro-Goldwyn-Mayer's animation unit to develop limited animation into a process that could answer television's need for quickly produced, cost-efficient children's fare. Hanna and Barbera developed the "Ruff and Ready" action-adventure shorts for airing on network television (NBC) beginning with the 1958 television year. A bit later, they sold a weekly package of "Huckleberry Hound," "Yogi Bear," and "Pixie and Dixie" cartoons to Kelloggs, which syndicated the program on local stations. A new world had opened for children's broadcasting. [22]

The Hanna-Barbera team was also instrumental in beginning a new trend in the length of television animation. Until the 1960s, cartoons on children's television were generally only a few minutes long. In addition to commercials, a half-hour series, such as "Mighty Mouse Playhouse" or "Boing Boing," needed three or four shorts and sometimes an extra performance by the host to complete the half hour. In 1960, however, Hanna-Barbera's "The Flintstones" appeared in prime time on ABC as a program for the family. Aside from being the first animated series made for prime time, "The Flintstones" also broke new ground in that each eipsode contained only one story that lasted the program's full half hour (including commercials). Barnouw notes that the limited animation technique used in the series was a bitter disappointment to many animators. The feeling was that in solving the financial problems of animation for television series through an assembly-line method, Hanna and Barbera had "sacrificed the medium [of animation]. Reducing lip movements to standardized cycles—vowel to vowel, ignoring consonants entirely—they made speech easy and cheap. This encouraged a heavy reliance on dialogue and developed a form of drama that, in spite of fanciful settings and time relationships, resembled acted telefilms."[23]

In other words, the arrival of limited animation on television opened the door for the imitation of television's live-action series. "The Flintstones," sold to advertisers as a family program during its initial airing, did not appear on children's television until its rebroadcast in 1968. However, two other Hanna-Barbera half-hour animated series, "Top Cat" and "The Jetsons," appeared regularly as part of the Saturday morning children's block as early as 1964-65. It is interesting that these earliest full-length limited animation series for television copied the plot lines of television's live-action adult situation comedies. "The Flintstones" was a takeoff on "The Honeymooners." "The Jetsons" was essentially "The Flintstones" transposed into the future. The major elements of "Top Cat" were taken from a Phil Silvers hit comedy of the 1950s, "You'll Never Get Rich." Beginning in the mid-1960s, however, the form of limited animation was used increasingly to imitate plot lines of action-adventure comic books, theatrical serials, and early network children's radio shows. In this connection, it is noteworthy that all of the action-adventure fantasies described earlier in this chapter were animated.

Limited animation programs were attractive to the networks because they could be produced more cheaply than nonstudio, live-action material and seemed to appeal to children. As the decade progressed, three firms (Hanna-Barbera, DePatie-Freling, and Filmation) created the lion's share of network children's series, in limited animation format. The situation was very profitable for them, as Muriel Cantor explained after interviewing the firms' producers in 1970.

> Although a producer of Saturday morning shows makes
> less money per program sold than does a producer of an
> evening film series, he is able to build a larger audience
> through word-of-mouth and good critical reviews. Even-
> ing television, while more lucrative, is also more risky.
> The profit is smaller for children's programs, and the

number of hours available for broadcasting them is smaller, but once a series is sold, the chance of failure is practically zero. Not only may such a series build an audience, but it is also more likely to be syndicated after being used a number of times by the network. Some children's shows can be revived often because their character is timeless and their audience changes constantly.[24]

Table 3.6 charts the growth of animation to a position of dominance in network children's television. The pattern of gradual movement in the early 1960s followed by an abrupt change after middecade is seen as clearly here as it was in some areas of subject matter. In 1960-61, 55 percent of the series had a live-action format, the same percentage as in 1958-59. Programs with animation alone, however, which had been climbing from a low of 2 percent in 1954-55 to 14 percent in 1958-59, climbed even higher to 23 percent in 1960-61. A steady increase in the percentage of animation over the next four years paralleled a decrease in the percentage of live action, so that,

TABLE 3.6

Live Action/Animation/Puppetry in Children's Series, 1960-69
(in percent)

|  | 1960-61 (N = 31) | 1962-63 (N = 29) | 1964-65 (N = 34) | 1966-67 (N = 37) | 1968-69 (N = 49) |
|---|---|---|---|---|---|
| Live action | 55 | 52 | 41 | 14 | 10 |
| Puppetry | 0 | 3 | 3 | 3 | 0 |
| Animation | 23 | 31 | 47 | 81 | 86 |
| Live action puppetry | 7 | 3 | 3 | 0 | 0 |
| Live and animation | 7 | 3 | 0 | 0 | 0 |
| All three | 10 | 7 | 6 | 3 | 4 |
| Other | 0 | 0 | 0 | 0 | 0 |
| Total | 102 | 99 | 100 | 101 | 100 |
| Diversity index | .375 | .374 | .394 | .678 | .751 |

Note: Totals greater or less than 100 percent are due to rounding error.

Source: Compiled by the author.

in 1964-65, the percentage of programs with animation alone (47 percent) exceeded the percentage with live action alone (41 percent). The abrupt change came in 1966-67, when animation soared to encompass 81 percent of the programs, and live action plummeted to include a mere 14 percent of the series. In the last two-year span of the decade, 86 percent of the programs used animation only, while just 10 percent used a live-action format.

This tremendous shift toward animation in the late 1960s is reflected in the sharp rise of the diversity index in Table 3.6 during 1966-67 and 1968-69. What should be stressed about this low level of diversity is that, during the last four years of the decade, no series mixed puppetry and live action and only two ("Banana Splits" and "Captain Kangaroo") mixed live action, animation, and puppetry. The proportion of series with puppets alone was no different from the very small percentage established in the late 1950s. The entire 1960s included only two puppet shows—"Burr Tilstrom's Kukla, Fran, and Ollie" and "Fireball XL-5." However, the almost complete absence of mixed formats marked a substantial departure from the previous decade. In 1950-51, 20 percent of the network children's series mixed live action with puppetry or animation or both. In 1958-59, 27 percent of the programs used mixed formats. In 1960-61 that figure dropped to 24 percent; in 1962-63 it declined to 13 percent; and in 1964-65 it fell to 9 percent, before dropping further to around 3 percent in the two-year spans that ended the decade.

One important reason for the decline of programs mixing live action, animation, and puppetry was the growth of half-hour animated films. Recall that, in the 1950s, many mixtures of format occurred in series in which a host supplemented the running of old theatricals with discussions of the films or antics of his "gang." This practice declined in the next decade as action-adventure cartoons increasingly fit the established half-hour durations of children's programs. Moreover, even programs that presented several (related or unrelated) cartoon segments tended to either have no host (for example, "Road Runner," "Super President," and "Tennessee Tuxedo and His Tales") or to have an animated host ("Mighty Mouse Playhouse," "Milton the Monster," and "Matty's Funday Funnies," for example).

The increased domination of network children's series by presentations with no host at all is indicated in Table 3.7. Following the pattern observed earlier, the absence of a host characterized roughly the same proportion of shows in the early 1960s as in the late 1950s (around 40 percent) and then jumped higher (to 61 percent) in 1964-65. The end of the decade saw an even greater proportion of programs with no hosts—81 percent in 1966-67 and 90 percent in 1968-69. Among them, series using a single presentation (mostly a full-length animated adventure) were dominant. Unhosted programs with several

TABLE 3.7

Presentation Methods on Children's Series, 1960–69
(in percent)

| | 1960–61 (N = 31) | 1962–63 (N = 29) | 1964–65 (N = 34) | 1966–67 (N = 37) | 1968–69 (N = 49) |
|---|---|---|---|---|---|
| Unhosted | | | | | |
| Single drama* or nonfiction | 32 | 21 | 32 | 43 | 61 |
| Several dramas or nonfiction | 10 | 17 | 29 | 38 | 29 |
| Hosted | | | | | |
| Host with gang, drama or non-fiction | 7 | 11 | 9 | 8 | 2 |
| Host without gang, drama or nonfic-tion | 16 | 14 | 6 | 5 | 4 |
| Talk show | 0 | 3 | 0 | 0 | 0 |
| Demonstration | 13 | 17 | 9 | 3 | 0 |
| Quiz show | 3 | 0 | 3 | 0 | 0 |
| Variety show (no regular drama) | 13 | 10 | 6 | 0 | 0 |
| Concert | 7 | 7 | 3 | 3 | 2 |
| Nonquiz competi-tion | 0 | 0 | 3 | 0 | 2 |
| Other | 0 | 0 | 0 | 0 | 0 |
| Total | 101 | 100 | 100 | 100 | 100 |
| Diversity index | .183 | .149 | .213 | .340 | .459 |

*Drama includes any performance that tells a story, whether live or recorded, studio or nonstudio based.

Note: Totals greater than 100 percent are due to rounding error.

Source: Compiled by the author.

presentations (often several cartoons) rose from 10 percent of the shows at the start of the decade to 38 percent in 1966-67, before dropping to 29 percent at decade's end.

In contrast to the increase in unhosted shows, hosted series decreased markedly throughout the decade. This decrease encompassed all the "host-affiliated" categories in Table 3.7, from a host with a gang presenting dramatic or nonfictional material to a variety show. Actually, the "host with a gang" category increased from 7 percent in the late 1950s to 11 percent in the early 1960s, but then it dropped to a barely visible 2 percent in 1968-69. Similarly, demonstration programs increased in the early 1960s but disappeared at decade's end. The other formats gradually edged from view during the decade. Interestingly, as some previously prominent formats progressively lost ground in the early 1960s while unhosted programs held their own or increased, a broad spread of presentation formats could be found among the network children's series. In fact, Table 3.7's diversity index indicates that 1962-63 (the years of the Minow and Dodd controversies) involved a broader distribution of categories than any previous two-year span. By the late 1960s, however, this situation was reversed as the unhosted formats gained virtually complete domination over the schedule. In 1966-67 and 1968-69, diversity in presentation formats reached its lowest point since 1948-49.

Earlier pages have already described several programs that used unhosted presentations, the dominant presentation format of the 1960s. It might now be interesting to sample series using other approaches. For example, "host with gang introducing drama or nonfiction" characterized several programs, particularly during the early part of the decade. Examples of series with this format were "Captain Kangaroo" (in which Mr. Green Jeans, Mr. Moose, and others joined the Captain in introducing various fiction and nonfiction segments), "Discovery" (in which hosts Frank Buxton and Virginia Gibson used a baby bloodhound and an otter to provide continuity between different program episodes), and the first "Bugs Bunny Show" (in which host Dick Coughlin and his puppets introduced Bugs Bunny cartoons). Hosts without gangs appeared in, among other programs, "Exploring" (in which Albert Hibbs presented such subjects as language, music, mathematics, and social studies through animation, puppetry, and live action), "Animal Secrets" (in which Loren Eisley introduced and narrated films), and "Matty's Funday Funnies" (in which animated hosts, Matty and Sisterbelle, introduced Beany and Cecil cartoons).

As for children's series with a variety format, seven appeared in the 1960s—"Paul Winchell Show" (a holdover from the previous decade), "Pip the Piper" (in which a fantasyland served as a backdrop for various performances in both CBS and ABC versions of the series),

"The Shari Lewis Show," "Lunch with Soupy Sales," "Magic Midway," and "Mr. Mayor." "The Shari Lewis Show" involved dance routines, songs, and banter built around a different theme each week and performed by the host (Shari), her puppet personalities (Lamb Chops, Charlie Horse, and Hush Puppy), and human members of the cast. "Lunch with Soupy Sales" also involved puppetry, with characters named White Fang, Black Tooth, and Willie the Worm. However, much more than in "Shari Lewis," the emphasis was on slapstick (including pie tossing) and absurd comic routines involving the host. "Magic Midway," a throwback to the circus-variety series of the 1950s, generated excitement in a different manner. Much quieter was "Mr. Mayor," starring Bob Keesham, who also played the title character in "Captain Kangaroo." Revolving around the activities of a fictional town, "Mr. Mayor" emphasized music, song, dance, and skitlike "visits" from continuing characters.

Seven "demonstration" series appeared during the 1960s, most of them during the early part of the decade. "Watch Mr. Wizard," the mainstay of the demonstration format, lasted through 1966-67. The other demonstration shows in this serious vein were "One, Two Three—Go!" (NBC's imitation of CBS's "Let's Take a Trip" from the 1950s), "Science All-Stars" (in which elementary and high school students exhibited their projects), and "Zoorama" (which took the viewer on tours of the San Diego Zoo). The more lighthearted demonstration series dealt with magic. "Magic Ranch" used a western set in which three young magician-hosts demonstrated various tricks, and "Magic Land of Allakazam" (in CBS and ABC versions) used the backdrop of a magic kingdom for illusions performed by Mark Wilson with the help of his wife, son, and others.

Only one concert series aired—the nonweekly "Young People's Concerts" begun in the late 1950s. It appeared throughout the decade. The one talk show that appeared was broadcast only during the 1963 television year. Called "Reading Room," it involved a host (Ned Hoopes) discussing a different book each week with several children and the book's author or some authority on its subject. Slightly more numerous than concerts and talk shows were quiz shows; two such series appeared. "On Your Mark" had host Sonny Fox asking youngsters questions that, if answered correctly, entitled them to work as reporters, mayors, or police for a day. "Do You Know?" involved two teams of 12-year-olds competing to answer questions about literature. Another uncommon program approach during the 1960s was the nonquiz competition. The networks broadcast only three competitive game series in the decade. "Video Village Junior," based on an adult game show called "Video Village," featured host Monty Hall directing two players through a giant game-board "village" strewn with gambling equipment with which they were to compete. "Shenanigans," a bit less mercenary, placed two competing children on a giant game board and had them progress toward the winner's position by completing various stunts or chores. "Storybook Squares," a spin-off from the adult "Hollywood Squares," dressed nine celebrities as children's storybook characters on the squares of a giant ticktacktoe board. Two children competed for a win in ticktacktoe by trying to determine whether the celebrities' answers to questions on topics relating to children were true or false.

The emphasis the past few pages have placed on various presentation formats with hosts should not obscure the fact that unhosted programs dominated network children's fare from middecade onward, so that, by 1968-69, 90 percent of the series had no hosts. This domination, a sharp reversal from the 1950s (when hosted shows were the rule), paralleled the rise of animated action-adventures as the standard approaches to network children's fare. Associated with this rise was the standardized presentation of series in nonstudio settings. The almost complete disappearance of studio-based programs after middecade was as sharp and dramatic as the fall of live-action programming during the same period. From a high of 61 percent of the series in 1952-53, studio-based programming had fallen to 21 percent in 1958-59. The early 1960s, possibly because of the temporary pressures for diversity urged by Senator Dodd and FCC Chairman Minow, saw an increase to 23 percent in 1960-61 and 38 percent in 1962-63. The next two-year span experienced a drop to 24 percent, but this provides no clue to the decrease in studio-based series that was to occur in the late 1960s. In 1966-67, studio series comprised 5 percent of all shows, and, in 1968-69, the figure fell to 4 percent.

As it did with subject matter, the Saturday morning children's block accentuated the dominant format patterns that were seen in programming as a whole during the 1960s. In the last four years of the decade, the overwhelming proportion of Saturday morning series was animated (about 90 percent), unhosted (about 93 percent), and nonstudio based (100 percent). Most programs with unusual formats (for example, "Animal World," "Young People's Concerts," "Storybook Squares," and "Discovery") tended to be placed outside of this most lucrative marketplace of children's television. The Saturday program schedule from 1969 presented in Figure 3.2 and the asterisks denoting Saturday morning shows from 1968 and 1969 in Appendix C attest to the growing uniformity of format in Saturday morning series.

Characterization

The nearly exclusive use of animation in network children's series by the late 1960s brought about some interesting changes in characterization from the previous decade. Recall that during the 1950s no less than 93 percent of the series had at least some humans (alone or with nonhumans) in the continuing cast. That percentage dropped rather sharply in the 1960s—to 80 percent in 1960-61, 58 percent in 1966-67, and 71 percent in 1968-69. The drop largely reflects the strong decrease in the percentage of programs with humans only. In the 1950s, that figure declined from a high of around 75 percent from 1950-51 through 1954-55 to a low of 50 percent in 1958-59. This decline continued into the 1960s, as Table 3.8 indicates. Presumably because the use of animation allowed the easy depiction of animals or inanimate objects as humanlike, series with humans alone fell gradually from 48 percent of the shows in 1960-61 to 38 percent in 1964-65 and 27 percent in 1966-67.

Interestingly, programs with humans alone did rise to 41 percent of the total in 1968-69, as action-adventures involving supermen and superwomen (for example, "Fantastic Four," "Batman/Superman,"

TABLE 3.8

Nature of Continuing Characters, 1960-69
(in percent)

| | 1960-61 (N = 31) | 1962-63 (N = 29) | 1964-65 (N = 34) | 1966-67 (N = 37) | 1968-69 (N = 49) |
|---|---|---|---|---|---|
| Human | 48 | 44 | 38 | 27 | 41 |
| Animal | 0 | 0 | 6 | 8 | 4 |
| Anthropomorphic animal | 19 | 10 | 15 | 32 | 20 |
| Anthropomorphic inanimate | 0 | 0 | 3 | 0 | 4 |
| Human and anthropomorphic | 13 | 31 | 24 | 26 | 20 |
| Human and animal | 19 | 14 | 12 | 5 | 10 |
| Other | 0 | 0 | 3 | 0 | 0 |
| No continuing cast | 0 | 0 | 0 | 0 | 0 |
| Total | 99 | 99 | 101 | 98 | 99 |
| Diversity index | .320 | .319 | .244 | .252 | .261 |

Note: Totals greater or less than 100 percent are due to rounding error.

Source: Compiled by the author.

and "Super Six") took hold. Nevertheless, a much wider variety of character types existed throughout the 1960s than the 1950s. The diversity index relating to the animal/human/inanimate aspect of characterization declined throughout most of the decade. The index was at all times lower than it was in the 1950s. As in the 1950s, series with only inanimate characters acting like humans were virtually nonexistent. Moreover, shows mixing humans and animals ("Samson and Goliath" and "Fury," for example) hovered around the same percentages seen in the previous decade. But series populated with only anthropomorphic continuing characters (for example, "George of the Jungle," "Peter Potamus," and "Linus the Lionhearted") strongly exceeded the low level of the previous decade. In addition, shows with both humans and anthropomorphic beings of any kind were more prevalent than in the 1950s. Saturday morning was a major site for these trends in the 1960s.

As implied earlier, another new trend in characterization that resulted from the increase in animation in the 1960s was the possession of superpowers by title characters. Recall that during the first decade of commercial television the title characters of only three programs ("Mr. I Maginzation," "Gumby," and "Mighty Mouse Playhouse") exhibited extraordinary powers of some kind. The fact that two of these superheadliners were animated pointed toward the future. However, the change did not take place during the first half of the 1960s. Despite the gradual increase in fantasy and animation from 1960-61 through 1964-65, series headlining superheroes comprised only between 3 percent and 6 percent of the series. It was in the late 1960s that such programs overwhelmed network children's television. Paced by "Atom Ant," "Mighty Mouse and the Mighty Heroes," "Superman," and others, superhero action-adventure series jumped to 32 percent of all network children's series in 1966-67 and 43 percent in 1968-69. Again, Saturday morning programs paralleled these developments quite closely.

Saturday morning also paralleled developments regarding the sex of the title character or host. Following a trend begun in 1952-53, programs with women in those positions ranged between 3 percent and 7 percent in the early 1960s, programs with both women and men in those positions ranged between 3 percent and 0 percent, and programs with men alone in those positions ranged between 77 percent and 79 percent. Beginning with 1964-65, the percentage of programs having both men and women as title characters or hosts increased just a bit, to 5 percent. However, not a single program during the last six years of the decade saw a female alone as host or title character.

The situation was not much different in terms of the sex of children in the continuing cast. In 1964-65, no continuing cast had only girls, and, during the rest of the decade, the figure hovered around 3 percent. Actually, it was also true that neither boys alone nor boys and girls together showed up in high proportions of programs throughout the decade. Series with boys alone reached 32 percent in 1960-61 and 31 percent in 1962-63 (after ranging between 8 percent and 24 percent in the previous decade) but declined to 21 percent, 14 percent, and 16 percent during the rest of the decade. Girls and boys together appeared in 7 percent of the series in 1960-61, 14 percent in 1962-63, and 15 percent in 1964-65 before their presence fell to 3 percent in 1966-67 and 1968-69. Paralleling these drops in the 1960s was a strong rise in the number of programs with no children at all. In the late 1950s, between 52 percent and 66 percent of the juvenile programs had no children in the regular cast. By contrast, in 1966-67 and 1968-69, 82 percent and 80 percent of the network programs for children had no continuing child characters. On Saturday morning, those figures were 80 percent and 77 percent, respectively.

## THE SHAPE OF PROGRAMMING

The very small percentage of shows with children in the continuing cast is yet another example of standardization—and the general diminishing of diversity—in network children's series by the late 1960s. Through these changes, regular network children's television rapidly took on an identifiable shape. The number of series per two-year span was not very stable in the decade, but the series' standard duration and placement in adjacent time periods gave children's television a "size" of some note. By 1969 the overwhelming number of shows for children was strung together by each network in half-hour bits from 9:00 A.M. to 12:30 P.M.

The "style" the children's block developed combined elements of children's radio adventures with elements of theatrical cartoons and comic books. Fiction was the rule, fantasy was the rule, and the emphasis within those areas was on action-adventure, where the hero (or heroes) weekly battled evil in one incarnation or another. The hero was, with very few exceptions, an adult male. Actually, even the nonadventure series had few females in title roles. Children in continuing casts were few and far between. Variety in ethnicity and race was also virtually nonexistent.

The overarching element of style in children's television was surely the animated nature of the programming. With over 80 percent of the series displaying the limited animation technique (nearly 90 percent on Saturday morning), cartoons became synonymous with children's television. Animation served as an umbrella that brought action-adventure and comic-chase series with different fictional subjects into a unified entity. From a network's standpoint, the advantage of creating such an entity was that the audience might treat it as a "block" to be viewed, rather than as a succession of unrelated shows. Such a programming strategy would then encourage the child audience to "flow" from one series to another. It would discourage switching stations or turning off the set. Furthermore, it would give the network high ratings compared with its competition, while providing the network's advertisers with many viewers for their commercials. A consequence of this perspective was that series not fitting the fictional, fantasy, action-oriented, animated style of the Saturday morning children's block tended to be produced in very small numbers (if at all) and to be isolated from the mainstream of juvenile programming. For example, all but one of the nonfiction series that appeared in the 1960s were scheduled away from Saturday morning.

Earlier pages have suggested the major influences that guided programming in this direction. Those influences were almost exclusively economic and related to concerns originating within the television industry itself. The fading of pressure from the public sector created an essentially laissez-faire atmosphere in which a "shape" for children's television could be created that rather uncompromisingly served the commercial needs of the networks and their advertisers. However, by the late 1960s, new pressures from outside the industry were beginning to develop. The pressures were attempting to force the networks to alter the shape they had created and expand the level of diversity they had achieved. The children's series the networks created in this new environment, and the way that programming responded to some pressures while maintaining the basic network requirements of "cost-efficient" fare and "audience flow," is a subject for the next chapter.

NOTES

1. Erik Barnouw, The Image Empire (New York: Oxford University Press, 1970), p. 201.

2. Ibid., p. 204.

3. Ibid., p. 198.

4. Quoted in Anthony M. Maltese, "A Descriptive Study of Children's Programming on Major American Television Networks from 1950 through 1964" (Ph.D. diss., Ohio University, 1967), p. 10.

5. William Melody, Children's Television: The Economics of Exploitation (New Haven, Conn.: Yale University Press, 1973), p. 49; and Newsweek, August 14, 1961, p. 66.

6. Barnouw, The Image Empire, p. 237.

7. Frank Orme, Television for the Family (Los Angeles: National Association for Better Radio and Television, 1965), p. 7.

8. Ibid.

9. Frank Orme and Betty Longstreet, "1968 TV Worst Yet for Children," Better Radio and Television 8 (Winter 1968): 1.

10. Muriel Cantor, "The Role of the Producer in Choosing Children's Television Content," in Television and Social Behavior, ed. G. A. Comstock and E. Rubinstein (Washington, D. C.: U.S. Government Printing Office, 1972), 1: 266.

11. Melody, Children's Television, p. 84.

12. Barry Cole and Mal Oettinger, Reluctant Regulators (Reading, Mass.: Addison-Wesley, 1978), pp. 249-50.

13. Ibid. , p. 250.

14. Barnouw, The Image Empire, p. 325.

15. Ibid. , p. 306.

16. Wendy Erlich, "Can Children's Television Programming Be Improved through Public Policy" (M.A. thesis, Annenberg School of Communications, University of Pennsylvania, 1973), p. 26.

17. Melody, Children's Television, p. 33.

18. Barnouw, The Image Empire, p. 150.

19. Melody, Children's Television, p. 45.

20. Ibid. , p. 46; and Lewis Jacobs, The Rise of the American Film: A Critical History, 2d ed. (New York: Teacher's College Press, 1968), p. 503.

21. Arthur Knight, The Liveliest Art (New York: Mentor, 1957), p. 268.

22. Niel Compton, "TV While the Sun Shines," Commentary, October, 1966.

23. Barnouw, The Image Empire, p. 206.

24. Cantor, "Role of the Producer," 1: 262.

# 4
## TOWARD A VIDEO MOSAIC, 1970-78

In the 1970s commercial network children's television experienced a moderation, and at the same time an extension, of some of the programming approaches established in the late 1960s. By 1978 Saturday morning programming, still the primary font of juvenile fare, had almost developed into a mosaic of various interrelated long and short program forms. This chapter will detail that development, suggest some factors influencing it, and explore its relationship to diversity.

### THE ECONOMIC AND SOCIAL ENVIRONMENT

In one striking way, the 1970s paralleled the 1960s. As in the previous decade, public and government interest in the subject was strongest at the beginning and end of the ten-year period. Unlike the 1960s, however, the storm that washed the public arena with controversial concerns about children's television did not blow over during middecade. No laissez-faire period gave network programmers time to set aside social demands and concentrate as completely as before on cost efficiency and audience flow in their juvenile market.

Perhaps the most important reason for this difference was Action for Children's Television (ACT), the group that had emerged on the national scene in 1969 as committed to changing programming aimed at youngsters. During its earliest days, the organization concentrated on local (Massachusetts) broadcasting problems. However, in the fall of 1969, representatives of the group appeared at Senator Pastore's hearing, which was investigating the relationship between television and juvenile delinquency. A bit later, they approached the FCC, testifying at its cable policy hearings and at hearings on the

ascertainment of community needs by broadcasters. ACT moved
closer to a national spotlight at the start of 1970, when key members
met with network officials (at CBS) for the first time and subsequently
gave their first interview to the New York Times.[1]

ACT consistently complained about the overcommercialization
of children's television. ACT members had at first been catalyzed
by their concern with violence in children's fare, the issue that has
historically drawn attention to the medium. In time, however, they
decided that the violence and low quality they perceived in children's
television was ultimately traceable to a "dismissal" of children by the
television industry as "simply . . . a market—a group of naive little
consumers."[2] Once this basic premise developed, ACT's goal became the alteration, and eventual elimination, of advertising in television programming aimed at children.

Dissatisfied with their reception at the networks (ABC and NBC
had even refused to meet with them), ACT officials petitioned the FCC
in February 1970 with three major recommendations: that no sponsorship or commercials be allowed on children's programs; that per-
formers and hosts be forbidden to use or sell products during children's programs; and that each station be required to provide a minimum of 14 hours per week of children's programming, divided into
age-specific groupings. About a year later, after much wrangling,
the commission voted to launch an inquiry into the advisability of im-
plementing ACT's recommendations.[3] Although the points ACT raised
had little directly to do with the nature of network or local children's
programming, this first FCC inquiry into children's television opened
a Pandora's box of issues, among them the extent of diversity in juvenile fare.

This is not the place to review the political intricacies leading
to the FCC's 1974 policy statement regarding ACT's petition. Barry
Cole and Mal Oettinger, in their book Reluctant Regulators, have detailed the nervous bargaining that went on within the commission, and
between the commissioners and broadcast-industry representatives.
In the end, they worked out a compromise wherein the National Association of Broadcasters would reduce the number of minutes per hour
its code allowed for commercials on children's television from 16 to
9.5. The FCC's policy statement, in turn, would not propose specific restrictions on commercials. The commissioners realized that
three years of testimony and letter writing to the FCC practically
compelled the commission to write something in the policy statement
about the clearly low level of scheduling and subject diversity in children's television during the late 1960s and early 1970s. Yet, with the
notable exception of Benjamin Hooks, they were afraid of giving the
impression that the FCC intended to specify programming requirements.[4] Thus, in the end, the policy statement reminded broadcasters

of their "responsibility to provide diversified programming designed to meet the varied needs and interests of the child audience. " In accomplishing its goal to "further the educational and cultural development" of youngsters, the commission noted as unfortunate the tendency "on the part of many stations to confine all or more of their children's programming to Saturday and Sunday mornings. " But the FCC indicated that it trusted industry self-regulation to remedy the situation. The commission expressed a "belief" that, in the future, stations should telecast "a reasonable amount of programming designed to educate and inform—and not simply to entertain"—that is, "programs with an educational goal in mind. "[5]

ACT was not pleased with the policy statement. Its president, Peggy Charren, suggested that "it is not enough to rely on the sense of commitment of broadcasters. If it were, ACT would not have come into existence. "[6] Nevertheless, the FCC inquiry represented the commission's first foray into the entire issue of children's television. The inquiry was also the last on the subject carried out by the FCC during the years covered by this study. It is worth noting, though, that, in July 1978 (the tail end of the 1978 television year), the commission reactivated its investigation of the subject and established a Children's Television Task Force. The purpose was to determine whether broadcasters were adhering to the 1974 policies. A year and a half later, the task force concluded that broadcasters were complying with the advertising policies suggested in 1974 but not with the programming guidelines. It presented the commission with a controversial range of regulatory options to consider—from taking no further action, to encouraging the development of new technologies (such as cable television and subscription television) that would likely give increased attention to the specialized child audience, to establishing mandatory children's programming rules for present-day broadcasters. [7]

ACT became involved in this second round of hearings on children's television as well. However, the organization's members were never content to pressure broadcasters only through the FCC. They also used other government agencies. For example, in 1971 and 1977, ACT presented petitions to the Federal Trade Commission with the aim of prohibiting vitamin and toy advertising to children. [8] In addition, ACT's attempts to change the medium were not limited to petitioning regulatory agencies directly. Much more than had any previous group interested in reshaping children's television, it attempted to spread opinions and garner support through wide-ranging public relation campaigns aimed at the general public and academia. In an early example of ACT's penchant for general publicity, the group sponsored a rally near the Plaza Hotel in New York and gave away balloons to children and pens with envelopes to their parents along

with advice on how to write the FCC.[9] The group's desire to connect
with academic and intellectual circles and encourage research on children's relation to television also took flight early in the organization's
life. In October 1970 ACT held the First National Symposium on the
Effects on Children of Television Programming and Advertising. In
doing so, ACT showed its ability to attract and organize academic and
industry leaders in the area. A book developed from the symposium,
the first of several books or reports for the general public, researchers, and the industry that the organization initiated during the decade.[10] Other ACT symposia followed. ACT also commissioned research on children's television.[11]

Although Action for Children's Television blazed new paths in
applying pressure to broadcasters and government agencies, it was
certainly not alone in agitating for more diversity in commercial network children's programs during the 1970s. While mainly stressing
their abhorrence of violence or commercialism on children's television, the national Parent-Teacher Association, American Medical
Association, Citizens' Communication Center, Nader's Center for the
Study of Responsive Law, National Association for Better Broadcasting (NABB—formerly NAFBRAT), and others did often state that their
ultimate goal was to broaden the scope of programming aimed at children. Occasionally, the organizations worked together on national
and local levels. An example of local cooperation took place in De-
cember 1971, when ACT joined the NABB, the Mexican-American Political Association, and the San Fernando Valley Fair Housing Council
in filing a petition asking the FCC to deny the license renewal appli-
cation of Channel 11 in Los Angeles. The petition, whose legal aspects were handled by the Citizens Communications Center, charged,
among other things, that the nonnetwork station broadcast an inordinate
number of old and violence-ridden children's programs.[12]

An example of cooperation on the national level involved the annual program guide compiled by the NABB. During much of the 1970s,
the NABB received aid from the Los Angeles PTA in compiling the
guide. ACT helped to publicize the guide by reprinting the 1974 version in its Family Guide to Children's Television. As in the 1960s,
NABB evaluations tended to concentrate on commercial network fare.
Throughout the 1970s the organization maintained that "the majority
of superior programs for children are still broadcast on public television," and it tended to lambast network series aimed at youngsters.
Here are examples of favorable and unfavorable reviews written during the 1978 television year.

> ABC Afterschool Specials—monthly, afternoons. Prob-
> ably the best entertainment for children available any-
> where in TV. Producer Martin Tahse is an expert and

conscientious craftsman. The stories are relevant and
entertaining, constructed so as to appeal to the audience
and make a point. For junior high level; well worth
family time.

Captain Kangaroo—CBS, daily. It takes four or five years
for small-fry to grow into and grow out of "Captain Kangaroo," and Bob Keeshan as the Captain has done a super job
of befriending many millions of the nation's children through
the cycles of their formative years. Warm and timely,
changing with the times, the program retains constant
values in content and production.

The Pink Panther—NBC, Saturdays. Made by adults essentially for adults, this is stylish and funny, but often
unsuitable for children. Violence and crime themes;
bombs and explosives.

Super Friends and other "Super" shows. These are the
superheroes with their fantastic physical powers—Superman, Batman, Aquaman, and Wonderwoman. With invin-
cible force they "fight injustice, right that which is wrong,
and serve all mankind." When our institutions and constituted authorities are helpless we call on our Super Friends,
and delegate to them all of our responsibilities to protect
ourselves against a world full of weird menaces. We don't
need anything else. Everything is settled for us by the
violent use of super power. That's the message! We de-
liver it to our children everytime we permit them to
watch one of these shows. [13]

After the Federal Communications Commission handed down
its policy statement on ACT's petition in 1974, the direct threat to
the networks of government intervention from one potentially powerful quarter abated. (ACT did ask the court of appeals to rule that the
FCC did not go far enough in the policy statement. It lost that appeal
in 1977.) Nevertheless, pressures upon the networks from ACT and
other groups continued throughout the 1970s. And, in 1977, a Federal Trade Commission staff report urged the commission to selec-
tively ban advertising to children of different ages. [14]

Broadcasters' public responses to threats against their autonomy
in children's programming varied. Early in the decade, NBC and CBS
acted to show their concern for the child audience by moving responsibility for juvenile material from the networks' daytime schedulers
to a separate children's programming department. ABC had already
founded one during the Minow years. [15] The National Association of
Broadcasters argued against the ACT petition by stressing that re-

search did not fully support ACT's conclusions about television's influence on youngsters and by arguing the value of self-regulation by its code. CBS claimed commercial television had become a whipping boy for the general failings of U.S. education.[16] NBC called the petition self-defeating, asserting that good programming could not be created without strong advertising support.[17] Only ABC, in addition to supporting the usual defensive measures by the broadcast lobby, used a public forum to propose substantial changes in children's television. ABC network chief James Duffy, warning about "the clear and present danger" of government intervention, proposed abandoning regular ratings in the Saturday morning children's block and substituting studies aimed at determining children's motivations and attitudes. Duffy argued that substitution of psychological research for popularity ratings would redirect the emphasis in both buying and selling time for children's fare from quantity to quality. But NBC and CBS showed no interest in joining that crusade, and nothing ever came of it.[18]

Throughout the 1970s the networks found themselves in a vise created by conflicting pressures—by pressures to de-emphasize commercialism and provide "high quality," "educational" programming, on the one side, and, on the other, by pressures to maintain the lucrative profit center they had established in series aimed at youngsters and not allow the precedent of de-commercializing television. The discussion until now has emphasized the first side of this vise. The second vise was more traditional and certainly powerful as well. In 1972 an FCC study revealed that children's television brought each network millions of dollars in profits.[19] The networks garnered that bounty by ensuring a consistent group of participating advertisers relatively low costs in reaching children through a specialized marketplace. A small number of production houses (chiefly Depatie-Freling, Filmation, Hanna-Barbera, Krofft, and Scheimer-Prescott) became reliable, consistent suppliers. The average costs of series were essentially lowered even more through the networks' complete control over program scheduling. They practically guaranteed that, once ordered, a program would survive at least long enough to air repeats of each episode several times. This practice decreased the average cost of each episode (since its charges could be spread over several airings, rather than one or two) and increased both network and producer profits.


THE RANGE OF PROGRAMMING

It was in this environment of mixed and often conflicting pressures that network programmers aimed series at youngsters during the 1970s. The following pages will explore the implications their labors had for diversity from 1970 through 1978. In general, the programming patterns established during the late 1960s took hold in the 1970s as well, although with some noteworthy differences. For example, the overwhelming domination by particular categories relaxed somewhat, resulting in a moderate level of diversity compared with that of the late 1960s. In addition, the networks instituted novel scheduling and format procedures for some fiction and a few key nonfiction series, procedures that added a new style to Saturday morning programming. Viewing the emergence of that style in the context of conflicting pressures upon programmers leads to a suggestion of how the shape of regular network children's television in the 1970s contained within it a way to deal with both sides of the "vise" at the same time. Children's television bowed to pressures from outside the industry in a highly visible way, while, at the same time, essentially serving the more traditional interests of the networks and their sponsors.

Scheduling and Program Duration

The most straightforward way to approach the changes in program diversity and style that children's television experienced after the 1960s is to start by examining the primary building blocks of diversity and style—the number of children's series the networks aired and the number of weekly hours those shows took up. A comparison reveals that the turn of the decade brought a sharp rise in the number of series programmed in a two-year span. The rise actually began in 1968-69. The networks presented 34 children's series in 1964-65, 37 in 1966-67, and 49 in 1968-69. They followed that jump with 58 in 1970-71, 62 in 1972-73, 55 in 1974-75, and 56 in 1976-77. (The 43 in 1978 reflects material from one year only and should not be strictly compared with two-year spans regarding number of programs and weekly hours.) The same pattern was noted in terms of weekly hours. From 1960-61 through 1966-67, the networks together broadcast a high of 22.5 hours and a low of 20.16 hours per two-year period. In 1966-67 they aired 34 weekly hours of children's fare. In 1970-71 the number rose to 36.91 and hovered there through 1976-77. As Table 4.1 indicates, CBS was the consistent leader among the networks in number of series telecast during the two-year periods from 1970 through 1977. NBC quite consistently fell into third place behind ABC. The single year 1978 saw a change, with NBC airing the largest percentage of programs. Table 4.2 shows CBS leading throughout the decade in the number of weekly hours, as it had in the 1960s.

In suggesting reasons for this rise in the overall number of series and weekly hours in the new decade, it is too easy to emphasize

## TABLE 4.1

Distribution of Children's Series by Networks, 1970–78
(in percent)

|  | 1970–71 (N = 58) | 1972–73 (N = 62) | 1974–75 (N = 55) | 1976–77 (N = 56) | 1978 (N = 43) |
|---|---|---|---|---|---|
| ABC | 36 | 36 | 35 | 33 | 26 |
| CBS | 40 | 37 | 44 | 35 | 33 |
| NBC | 24 | 28 | 22 | 33 | 42 |
| Total | 100 | 101 | 101 | 101 | 101 |

Note: Totals greater than 100 percent are due to rounding error.

Source: Compiled by the author.

## TABLE 4.2

Weekly Hours Taken Up by Children's Series, 1970–78

|  | 1970–71 | 1972–73 | 1974–75 | 1976–77 | 1978 |
|---|---|---|---|---|---|
| ABC | 11.50 | 11.75 | 10.08 | 11.08 | 7.38 |
| CBS | 17.91 | 16.58 | 16.08 | 16.50 | 13.33 |
| NBC | 7.50 | 8.00 | 6.50 | 8.50 | 9.50 |
| Total | 36.91 | 36.33 | 32.66 | 36.08 | 30.21 |

Note: The table does not include series scheduled less than once a week.

Source: Compiled by the author.

91

TABLE 4.3

Scheduling of Children's Programs, 1970-78
(in percent)

| | 1970-71 (N = 58) | 1972-73 (N = 62) | 1974-75 (N = 55) | 1976-77 (N = 56) | 1978 (N = 43) |
|---|---|---|---|---|---|
| Monday-Friday | | | | | |
| Morning (7:00-11:30) | 2 | 2 | 2 | 2 | 2 |
| Afternoon (12:00-4:00) | 0 | 0 | 0 | 0 | 0 |
| Early evening (4:30-7:00) | 0 | 0 | 0 | 0 | 0 |
| Prime time (7:00 P.M.-11:00 P.M.) | 0 | 0 | 0 | 0 | 0 |
| Friday alone | | | | | |
| Morning | 0 | 0 | 0 | 0 | 0 |
| Afternoon | 0 | 0 | 0 | 0 | 0 |
| Early evening | 0 | 0 | 0 | 0 | 0 |
| Prime time | 0 | 0 | 0 | 0 | 0 |
| One weekday (not Friday) | | | | | |
| Morning | 0 | 0 | 0 | 0 | 0 |
| Afternoon | 0 | 2 | 2 | 4 | 5 |
| Early evening | 0 | 0 | 0 | 0 | 0 |
| Prime time | 0 | 0 | 0 | 0 | 0 |
| Two to four weekdays | | | | | |
| Morning | 0 | 0 | 0 | 0 | 0 |
| Afternoon | 0 | 0 | 0 | 0 | 0 |
| Early evening | 0 | 0 | 0 | 0 | 0 |
| Prime time | 0 | 0 | 0 | 0 | 0 |
| Saturday | | | | | |
| Morning | 69 | 63 | 66 | 60 | 51 |
| Afternoon | 21 | 16 | 13 | 20 | 28 |
| Early evening | 0 | 0 | 0 | 0 | 0 |
| Prime time | 0 | 0 | 0 | 0 | 0 |
| Sunday | | | | | |
| Morning | 7 | 11 | 11 | 9 | 7 |
| Afternoon | 2 | 2 | 2 | 0 | 0 |
| Early evening | 0 | 0 | 2 | 2 | 2 |
| Prime time | 0 | 0 | 0 | 0 | 0 |
| One weekday and Saturday | | | | | |
| Morning/morning | 0 | 0 | 0 | 0 | 0 |
| Evening/morning | 0 | 0 | 0 | 0 | 0 |
| Other time combination | 0 | 0 | 0 | 0 | 0 |
| One weekday and Sunday | | | | | |
| Morning/morning | 0 | 0 | 0 | 0 | 0 |
| Evening/morning | 0 | 0 | 0 | 0 | 0 |
| Other time combination | 0 | 0 | 0 | 0 | 0 |
| Multiple weekday and Saturday | | | | | |
| Morning/morning | 0 | 0 | 0 | 0 | 0 |
| Evening/morning | 0 | 0 | 0 | 0 | 0 |
| Other time combination | 0 | 0 | 0 | 0 | 0 |
| Multiple weekday and Sunday | | | | | |
| Morning/morning | 0 | 0 | 0 | 0 | 0 |
| Evening/morning | 0 | 0 | 0 | 0 | 0 |
| Other time combination | 0 | 0 | 0 | 0 | 0 |
| Saturday and Sunday | | | | | |
| Morning/morning | 0 | 0 | 0 | 0 | 0 |
| Evening/morning | 0 | 0 | 0 | 0 | 0 |
| Other time combination | 0 | 3 | 4 | 4 | 5 |
| Total | 101 | 99 | 102 | 101 | 100 |
| Diversity index | .526 | .437 | .468 | .412 | .349 |

Note: Totals greater or less than 100 percent are due to rounding error.

Source: Compiled by the author.

extraindustry pressure—for example, the Pastore hearings and the ACT petition. The nature of the increase suggests that the primary motive was simply to further develop and extend the Saturday morning children's block and its adjacent afternoon slot. In the early and mid-1960s, the networks began their children's series at 9:00 or 10:00 on Saturday morning. By the 1970s all were beginning at 8:00 A.M., thus adding an hour or two to the children's schedule. Moreover, the networks were pushing out the boundaries of their Saturday afternoon children's programming somewhat, from 1:00 or 1:30 P.M. to past 2:00.

Saturday morning remained the primary repository of network children's series from 1970 through 1978. As Table 4.3 indicates, the time slot contained over 60 percent of all children's programs through 1976-77, around the same proportion as in the late 1960s. In 1978, 51 percent of the children's series appeared on Saturday morning. It is doubtful that this downturn reflects a drop in the time period's importance. More probably, it relates to 1978's status as a one-year rather than two-year span; that is, 1978 could not reflect the extra series that were typically added in the second year.

As in the late 1960s, the period that held the second-largest number of children's programs during the 1970s was Saturday afternoon. Sunday morning was in third place with from 7 to 11 percent of the programs. Saturday morning, Saturday afternoon, and Sunday morning thus encompassed over 86 percent of all the network children's series. In 1970-71, in fact, only two series aired outside those three slots. One of the series was "Captain Kangaroo." Cut back from six to five days a week, it ran Monday through Friday on CBS throughout the 1970s. The other program, also on CBS, was "Young People's Concerts," telecast a few times a year on Sunday afternoons. After 1970-71 four other programs appeared outside the top three time periods. Two, CBS's "Family Classics" and "Festival of the Lively Arts," aired on Sundays in the early evening. The others, ABC's "Afterschool Special" and NBC's "Special Treat," were shown once a month on a weekday afternoon.

The diversity index in Table 4.3 reflects the narrowness of scheduling in the 1970s. Comparing its index with those of Tables 2.3 and 3.4 reveals that the two-year spans in the 1970s had a consistently lower level of scheduling diversity than existed from 1948-49 through 1958-59 or from 1960-61 through 1968-69. In fact, in 1970-71, there was less scheduling diversity than at any time from 1948-49 through 1978. While diversity increased somewhat after 1970-71, its level in the two-year spans that followed was always lower than at any time before 1964-65.

The most unusual scheduling practice of the 1970s took place in weekend children's programming. The years from 1970-71 through

1978 witnessed "information spot" series—umbrella titles referring to five-minute segments that were inserted between other shows on the Saturday morning, Saturday afternoon, and Sunday morning schedules. This practice of lacing short segments throughout the lineup was new for the commercial television networks. It started with CBS's introduction of "In the Know" during the 1971 television year, the year coinciding with the start of the FCC children's hearings. The basic theme of "In the Know"—noting various happenings in various parts of the world—was not new. "Watch the World" with John Cameron Swayze and family had used the idea in 1950 and 1951. The novelty of "In the Know" lay in its duration and scheduling approach. CBS produced the live-action series (and "In the News," its successor) with animated titles in unrelated five-minute segments. It presented those segments at 55 minutes after certain hours during Saturday morning and afternoon. The same scheduling and duration policy was adopted by ABC during the 1973 season.

ABC chose the subject of arithmetic, called its series "Multiplication Rock," and added an innovation of its own—complete animation. The network focused on language with its "Multigrammar Rock" during 1974-75 and, in 1976-77 and 1978, used the "Schoolhouse Rock" title to encompass different kinds of educational spots. As will be seen, these spots represented a key change in the networks' approach to nonfiction programming and, ultimately, to programming as a whole. *

Of more immediate interest is the fact that the information spots were among the few series from 1970 through 1978 that aired more than once a week. CBS telecast different segments of "In the Know" five times on Saturday in 1971, and, in subsequent years, ABC and CBS aired information spots more than seven times during the Saturday and Sunday children's blocks. In general, though, the networks followed the pattern established in the 1960s of scheduling around 90 percent of the programs on a weekly basis. In 1970-71, 95 percent of the shows aired once a week. In the two-year spans and final year that followed, 90 percent, 87 percent, 89 percent, and 88 percent of the programs were telecast weekly.

Coupled with the continued domination of weekly series was the continued use of the half-hour length for a majority of shows. How-

---

*The only previous example of a children's program duration of less than 15 minutes was "Burr Tillstrom's Kukla, Fran, and Ollie," the five-minute, Monday-through-Friday anomaly of 1962-63. It might also be noted that, while the information spots were novelties on commercial television, short segments similar in format to "Schoolhouse Rock" and "In the Know" had formed the core of public television's "Sesame Street" beginning with the 1970 television year.

ever, the late 1970s saw a fairly substantial departure from nearly total blanketing of children's television with 30-minute programs that had begun in the previous decade. While 95 percent of the series in 1966-67 fit the half-hour mold, and from 86 percent to 81 percent of the series in the two-year spans immediately following had that length, the number of half-hour programs dropped to 76 percent in 1976-77 and 65 percent in 1978. The slight drop at the turn of the decade was due to the appearance of the five-minute information spots. The sharper drop in the percentage of half-hour programs after middecade accompanied a rise in hour-long shows—from 15 percent in the early 1970s to 20 percent and 29 percent in 1976-77 and 1978, respectively. In fact, the late 1970s saw more programs exceeding a half-hour than any time since the start of commercial children's television. This increase took hold on Saturday morning in particular. Hour-long shows dropped from 15 percent of Saturday morning series in 1970-71 to 5 percent in 1974-75 but then rose sharply to 17 percent in 1976-77 and 35 percent in 1978. Accompanying the climb in hour-long shows in 1978 were series lasting longer than one hour. CBS lengthened "Bugs Bunny/Road Runner" from an hour to 90 minutes, and ABC telecast "Scooby's Laff-a-Lympics" for two hours on Saturday morning. (The increase in programs lasting an hour or more in space previously devoted to half-hour shows helps to further explain the drop in the number of series from 1976-77 to 1978.)

Several of the scheduling patterns that have been discussed are reflected in Figure 4.1, which records the New York Times television listings for a Saturday morning and afternoon in January 1970 and 1978. The Times did not indicate the information spots placed between the series listed in 1978. Scheduling those spots in 1978 but not 1970 made for an important difference in the overall "look" of the programming. This difference will be described in forthcoming pages. For the moment, however, discussion will center on only the series marked on the chart. For example, no difference appears in the "size" of the combined morning and afternoon children's blocks when 1970 is compared with 1978. In 1970 ABC and NBC began to follow CBS's policy of starting Saturday morning juvenile fare at 8:00 A.M. In 1969 those networks had started at 9:00 A.M. Moreover, in 1970 CBS and NBC extended their Saturday afternoon children's programming by 30 minutes over the previous decade. They followed the practice in 1978 as well. The consequence of lengthening both the morning and afternoon periods was that there were more total children's hours on Saturday in January 1970 and January 1978 than in January 1969—10 in 1969, 15 in 1970, and 15.5 in 1978.

A comparison of Figures 3.1 and 4.1 also reflects the increased duration of individual Saturday morning series by 1978. The number of shows that lasted longer than a half hour increased from three in

FIGURE 4.1

Saturday Morning and Afternoon Television, January 1970 and January 1978

January 10, 1970
Saturday Morning

7:00    Project Know (ABC) to 7:30
       Black Letters (CBS) to 7:30
       Colonel Bleep (NBC) to 7:30
7:30    Davey and Goliath (ABC) to 8:00
       Having a Ball (CBS) to 8:00
       Dodo (NBC) to 8:00
8:00    Adventures of Gulliver (ABC) to 8:30
       The Jetsons (CBS) to 8:30
       Heckle and Jeckle Show (NBC) to 9:00
8:30    Smokey the Bear (ABC) to 9:00
       Bugs Bunny/Road Runner (CBS) to 9:30
9:00    The Cattanooga Cats (ABC) to 10:00
       Here Comes the Grump (NBC) to 9:30
9:30    Dastardly and Muttley (CBS) to 10:00
       Pink Panther Show (NBC) to 10:00
10:00   Hot Wheels (ABC) to 10:30
       Perils of Penelope Pitstop (CBS) to 10:30
10:30   Hardy Boys (ABC) to 11:00
       Scooby-Doo (CBS) to 11:00
       Banana Splits (NBC) to 11:30
11:00   Skyhawks (ABC) to 11:30
       Archie Comedy Hour (CBS) to 12:00
11:30   George of the Jungle (ABC) to 12:00
       Jambo (NBC) to 12:00

January 10, 1970
Saturday Afternoon

12:00   Fantastic Voyage (ABC) to 12:30
       The Monkees (CBS) to 12:30
       The Flintstones (NBC) to 12:30
12:30   American Bandstand (ABC) to 1:30
       Wacky Races (CBS) to 1:00
       Underdog (NBC) to 1:00
1:00    Superman (CBS) to 1:30
       Agriculture USA (NBC) to 1:30
1:30    Island in the Sun (ABC) to 2:00
       Jonny Quest (CBS) to 2:00
       International Zone (NBC) to 2:00
2:00    Like It Is (ABC) to 3:00
       Opportunity Line (CBS) to 2:30
       Senior Bowl Football (NBC) to 2:30
2:30    Learning Experience (CBS) to 3:00
3:00    Pro Bowler's Tour (ABC) to 4:30
       Young World 70 (CBS) to 3:30
3:30    Ounce of Prevention (CBS) to 4:00

4:00    Golf Classic (CBS) to 6:00

January 18, 1978
Saturday Morning

7:00    PPT Magazine (ABC) to 7:30
       Patchwork (CBS) to 8:00
       A Better Way (NBC) to 7:30
7:30    Come Along (ABC) to 8:00
       Mr. Magoo (NBC) to 8:00
8:00    All New Superfriends Hour (ABC) to 9:00
       Skatebirds (CBS) to 9:00
       C.B. Bears (NBC) to 9:00

9:00    Scooby's Laff-a-Lympics (ABC) to 11:00
       Bugs Bunny/Road Runner (CBS) to 10:30
       Space Sentinels (NBC) to 9:30
9:30    Super Witch (NBC) to 10:00

10:00   Bang-Shang Lalapalooza (NBC) to 10:30

10:30   Batman/Tarzan (CBS) to 11:30
       I Am the Greatest (NBC) to 11:00
11:00   Krofft Supershow 78 (ABC) to 12:00
       Thunder (NBC) to 11:30
11:30   Space Academy (CBS) to 12:00
       Search and Rescue (NBC) to 12:00

January 18, 1978
Saturday Afternoon

12:00   Weekend Special (ABC) to 12:30
       Secrets of Isis (CBS) to 12:30
       Baggy Pants and the Nitwits (NBC) to 12:30
12:30   American Bandstand (ABC) to 1:30
       Fat Albert (CBS) to 1:00
       Red Hand Gang (NBC) to 1:00
1:00    What's New, Mr. Magoo? (CBS) to 1:30
       Positively Black (NBC) to 2:00
1:30    Eyewitness News Conference (ABC) to 2:00
       CBS Children's Film Festival (CBS) to 2:00
2:00    Education Update (ABC) to 2:30
       The People (CBS) to 2:30
       Not For Women Only (NBC) to 2:30
2:30    World Series of Auto Racing (ABC) to 3:30
       Eye On (CBS) to 3:00
       Journey to Adventure (NBC) to 3:00
3:00    Dating Game (CBS) to 3:30
       Tennis (NBC) to 3:30
3:30    Pro Bowler's Tour (ABC) to 4:30
       Golf (CBS) to 4:30
       College Basketball (NBC) to 6:00

Note: The underscored programs are network children's series. New York time is used.

Source: New York Times.

96

January 1969, to five in January 1970, to seven in January 1978.
NBC was not involved in this increase, but CBS and ABC were, with
a resulting decrease in the number of shows they telecast in the primary children's block. Excluding "In the News" (which is left out of
the Times schedule), CBS went from six series in 1969 and 1970 to
four in 1970. ABC's decrease was more dramatic. In January 1969
the network aired six series on Saturday morning; in January 1970 it
aired seven; and in January 1978, excluding "Schoolhouse Rock," it
aired only three—the hour-long "Super Friends," the two-hour "Scooby's Laff-a-Lympics," and the hour-long "Krofft Supershow 78."

Subject Matter

Accompanying the intrusion of hour-long programs and five-
minute spots into the mainstream juvenile block were changes in subject matter, format, and characterization that helped carry the diversity and shape of network children's television to a new stage by
the late 1970s.
In terms of the overall allocation of series dealing with fiction,
nonfiction, and performing activities, the differences between the late
1960s and the 1970s were slim. The networks continued to program
fiction in 80 percent to 90 percent of the series from 1970-71 through
1978. The percentage of fiction programming did drop a bit during
the 1970s, enough for nonfiction to rise slightly above its two-decade
low of 4 percent in 1968-69. Performing activities remained at the
low level of the late 1960s, generally hovering around 4 percent. As
in the previous decade, only "Captain Kangaroo" befuddled attempts
to classify it as fiction, nonfiction, or performing activities.
When the series are sorted by their main subjects, however,
greater differences emerge between programming in the 1960s and
the 1970s, as a comparison of Tables 3.5 and 4.4 shows. The slight
increase in nonfiction brought a scattering of subjects not seen during
the late 1960s, or any previous period for that matter. Series mixing
nonfiction topics (for example, "Discovery," "In the Know," and
"Curiosity Shop") were still the most consistently present nonfiction
fare. But the heretofore unknown activity of teaching the alphabet
and arithmetic on commercial television (through information spots
"Multigrammar Rock," "Multiplication Rock," or "Schoolhouse Rock")
also took to the airwaves on a continuing basis. Rarer, though just
as novel for commercial children's television, were programs on history ("You Are There" and the semifictional "Go—USA!") and biography
(the semifictional "U.S. of Archie"). Religion, seen in only one show
before the 1970s ("Exploring God's World" in 1954-55), appeared
once again around middecade in "Marshall Ephron's Illustrated,

TABLE 4.4

Main Subjects of Children's Series, 1970-78
(in percent)

| | 1970-71<br>(N = 58) | 1972-73<br>(N = 62) | 1974-75<br>(N = 55) | 1976-77<br>(N = 56) | 1978<br>(N = 43) |
|---|---|---|---|---|---|
| Fiction | | | | | |
| Storybook | 2 | 0 | 0 | 0 | 0 |
| Western | 0 | 0 | 0 | 0 | 0 |
| Police | 17 | 11 | 11 | 18 | 19 |
| Science fiction | 2 | 7 | 7 | 9 | 10 |
| Jungle or "wilds" | 3 | 0 | 5 | 7 | 2 |
| Other adventure | 37 | 51 | 47 | 24 | 25 |
| Adventure in different settings | 5 | 3 | 5 | 2 | 0 |
| Realistic problem drama | 2 | 5 | 5 | 11 | 12 |
| Unrelated dramatic sequences | 17 | 7 | 0 | 8 | 21 |
| Nonfiction | | | | | |
| ABCs, arithmetic | 0 | 2 | 2 | 2 | 2 |
| History | 2 | 0 | 0 | 2 | 0 |
| Geography | 0 | 0 | 0 | 0 | 0 |
| Nature | 3 | 0 | 0 | 2 | 2 |
| Other physical science | 0 | 2 | 0 | 0 | 0 |
| Occupations | 0 | 0 | 2 | 0 | 0 |
| Biography | 0 | 0 | 2 | 2 | 0 |
| Religion | 0 | 0 | 2 | 2 | 0 |
| Mixture nonfiction | 5 | 7 | 4 | 4 | 2 |
| Performing activities | | | | | |
| Child sports | 0 | 0 | 0 | 0 | 0 |
| Competitive games | 0 | 2 | 0 | 4 | 0 |
| Magic | 0 | 0 | 0 | 0 | 0 |
| Music | 2 | 2 | 2 | 0 | 0 |
| Various performances | 2 | 0 | 4 | 2 | 2 |
| Subject mixture | 2 | 2 | 2 | 2 | 2 |
| Total | 101 | 101 | 100 | 101 | 99 |
| Diversity index | .204 | .234 | .251 | .128 | .170 |

Note: Totals greater or less than 100 percent are due to rounding error.

Source: Compiled by the author.

98

Simplified, and Painless Sunday School" (1974-75 and 1976-77). Interestingly, "other physical science," a consistent category in the 1950s and 1960s, aired only in one two-year span of the 1970s, through a resurrection of "Watch Mr. Wizard" (1972-73).

The small number of programs featuring performing activities in the 1970s spread across three main subject areas, one more than in the late 1960s. CBS's "Young People's Concerts," which covered the music category from 1958-59 (with Leonard Bernstein and then Michael Tillson Thomas at the helm), continued its nonweekly run through 1974-75. In the years that followed, concerts for children appeared on CBS through the nonweekly "Festival of Lively Arts," an umbrella title for various kinds of performances. The only other series with various performances during the 1970s were "The Harlem Globetrotters Popcorn Machine" and "The Hudson Brothers Razzle Dazzle Comedy Show," fast paced mixtures of comic sketches, songs, and dance routines. Competitive games formed the third "performing" category seen in the decade. The programs were "Runaround," "Way Out Games," and "Junior Almost Anything Goes."

A wide variety of fiction appeared in the 1970s, as in the late 1960s. Specific comparisons between the main subjects of those periods reveal some rather small differences and some fairly large ones. One small difference worth noting involves the final disappearance of the western adventure from network children's television. Westerns had dropped from a high of 24 percent in the 1950s to 4 percent in 1968-69, but it was not until the 1970s that this former mainstay of children's adventure bit the dust. Not a single western was aired from 1970 through 1978. On the other hand, storybook programs, which disappeared in the late 1960s, did have one representative for two years during the 1970s. Called "Jambo," the series told folktales of African wildlife.

One subject area that had no representation from 1948-49 through 1968-69 appeared and grew in strength during the 1970s. "Realistic problem dramas"—plays dealing with everyday problems of children—became the "prestige" programming of the decade. At their peak, they numbered six shows, 11 percent of the programs in 1976-77. The first, "The CBS Children's Film Festival," presented hour-long films from around the world. It appeared weekly in 1970 and continued on that basis through 1978. The three other problem dramas that aired each week during the 1970s were half-hour shows that were made in the United States. Two, "Muggsy" (NBC) and "Fat Albert and the Cosby Kids" (CBS), focused on lower-class city life. "Fat Albert" depicted the escapades of black children growing up in North Philadelphia, according to the embellished reminiscences of host Bill Cosby. "Muggsy" explored life in an unidentified inner-city neighborhood through the eyes of Margaret ("Muggsy") Malloy, a 13-year-old orphan. "Weekend Special," a third program with realistic stories, was an anthology series that often presented dramas about different kinds of children at different levels of society. This approach was also used by two non-weekly programs—the hour-long "Afterschool Special" (ABC) and "Special Treat" (NBC). A common source for plots in those shows were children's books popular with junior high students. Some "Afterschool Special" dramas were serialized on "Weekend Special."

During the late 1960s, the most common series were adventures that did not fit western, police, science fiction, or jungle plot lines. Programs with unrelated dramatic sequences in each episode held a close second; adventures of police or law agents hugged third; and science fiction, jungle, and western fare straggled behind. The 1970s saw the general adventure still holding first place. In fact, it rose from 25 percent of the shows in 1968-69 to 51 percent in 1972-73, before falling to its former level at decade's end. Police shows were strongly evident. They dropped from their all-time high of 25 percent in 1968-69 but still generally represented about 17 percent of the fare. However, shows with unrelated dramatic sequences fell from 17 percent in 1970-71 to 0 percent in 1974-75, before surging to 21 percent (and second place again) in 1978. Consequently, police shows held second place among main subject categories throughout most of the decade. When unrelated dramatic sequences were uncommon, science fiction series grabbed third place. That category, which had dropped from 11 percent to 4 percent in the late 1960s, dropped further to 2 percent in 1970-71 before rising gradually to 10 percent in 1978. Wavering from 0 percent to 5 percent in the decade were series that aired a different kind of adventure in each episode. Note that this anthology category, which included "Scooby Doo Movies," "Saturday Superstar Movies," and "Family Classics" in the 1970s, excluded "Afterschool Special," "Special Treat," "CBS Children's Film Festival," and "Weekend Special" because, by prearranged priority, their emphasis on true-to-life stories about children dictated their entry as realistic drama.

Clearly, space does not allow even brief descriptions of all the children's fiction series aired by the commercial networks from 1970 through 1978. However, the strong rise in the early 1970s of programs that did not fit western, police, science fiction, or jungle themes should indicate that a substantial change in the general pattern of action took place during those years of FCC scrutiny. What happened was that the networks played down juvenile television's most controversial plot line—the action-adventure. Programs in which heroes pursued evil in their environment declined sharply in the early years of the decade—from 51 percent of the shows in 1968-69 to 26 percent in 1970-71 and 18 percent in 1972-73. Interestingly, this level of action-adventure programming roughly matched the level seen in the early 1960s, after the networks lowered the proportion of such series in response to the Minow-Dodd pressures against television violence. The late 1960s experienced a rise in action-adventure fare as those pressures diminished, and the 1970s followed this direction as well. In 1974-75—the time of the FCC's wrist-slapping report— action-adventures comprised 25 percent of network children's shows. However, in 1976-77, action-adventure accounted for 32 percent of the series, and in 1978 the use of this plot line returned to the 1966-67 level of 42 percent.

The manner in which the networks altered their program fare to diminish the number of action-adventure plot lines in the early 1970s suggests the distance they were willing to go and the risks they were willing to take in order to increase diversity and originality in their children's fare. That distance was not very great. The plot lines that substituted for action-adventure plot lines during the 1970s generally maintained the overall action orientation of children's television and deviated from that orientation only with approaches that seemed tried and true. Two approaches were particularly used to maintain a frenetic beat to children's television, despite the crop-off in the number of heroes pursuing villains. One technique that was in greatest use at middecade was the "man against nature" formula. Rather than have humanlike protagonists fighting other humanlike creatures, 15 "children's hour" series pitted human or humanlike heroes against the exciting, tension-filled dangers of nature in the raw. For example, "Land of the Lost" set a forest ranger and his children in a world of prehistoric creatures and watched them struggle to survive and escape. "Valley of the Dinosaurs" told the saga of a different family similarly transported into a dinosaur-infested past. "Emergency plus Four" depicted the work of a fire department's rescue squad. "Barrier Reef" followed a marine biologist, his son, and their crew as they explored the dangers of the great barrier reef off Australia. And "Scooby-Doo, Where Are You?" depicted the adventures of four teenagers and their easily frightened dog in their attempts to solve supernatural mysteries.

The comic-chase plot line was even more important than the "man against nature" formula in maintaining an action-oriented rhythm to children's fare while the networks held action-adventure at bay. This established escape-capture-escape motif was of particular importance in 1970-71 and 1972-73, when the networks were just beginning to present "man against nature" stories, and in 1978, when those stories faded and comic-chase routines complemented action-adventure series much as they had in the late 1960s. Most of the comic-chase programs (for example, "Bugs Bunny/Road Runner," "Tom and Jerry," and "Pink Panther") followed the tradition of such series from

the 1950s and 1960s. A few unrelated cartoons, often theatrical releases from the 1940s and 1950s, aired back to back, sometimes with
the title character as host. However, in the 1970s, a new kind of
comic-chase series emerged that brought the plot line closer to action-adventure. This new comic chase actually can be traced to a
series begun in 1968-69—"Wacky Races." Its episodes depicted a
seemingly endless cross-country automobile race and focused on the
illegal and colorful efforts of evil Dick Dastardly and his dog Muttley
to win. Aside from siring two direct spin-offs ("Dastardly and Muttley" and Perils of Penelope Pitstop"), "Wacky Races" seems to have
encouraged three other comic-chase programs involving races in the
1970s. "Around the World in 80 Days" followed an attempt by Phileas
Fogg to win a wager (and the hand of his love) by traveling around the
world in 80 days despite obstructions by evil Mister Fix. "Bailey's
Comets" told the saga of a skating team trying to win a transglobal
skating race in the face of diabolical schemes by other teams to elimi-
nate them. Finally, "Yogi's Space Race" involved Yogi Bear and
friends in comic competition.

The calmer shows that, particularly in the early 1970s, dotted
this action-filled environment were generally unusual only because
they were calmer. True, some of the shows were genuine novelties
for television. "Here Comes the Grump" and "H. R. Pufnstuf," for
example, contributed the air of fairy tales to the children's lineup.
But the majority of series that did not emphasize action-adventure,
comic chases, or man against nature went no further than theatrical
films, comic books, or adult television comedies in reaching for ideas
that could be transmogrified into children's series. Thus, for example, "The New Adventures of Gilligan" continued the comic saga of
"Gilligan's Island"'s shipwrecked population; "The Brady Kids" continued the story of "The Brady Bunch," with emphasis on the youngsters; and "The Barkleys" copied the popular "All in the Family,"
using humanlike dogs as the main characters. These programs were
ABC or NBC series. CBS, for its part, tended to concentrate on using the well-known "Archie" comic book characters in several situation comedies beginning in 1968-69—"The Archie Show," "Archie's
Funhouse," "Archie Comedy Hour," "Everything's Archie," "Archie and Sabrina," "Sabrina the Teen-Age Witch," and "Sabrina and
the Groovie Goolies."

It is important to note that this technique of using the same
characters in different programs was not limited to CBS, nor to non-
action programs. Actually, a good part of the children's schedule in
the 1970s was created by renaming and repackaging children's series
that had aired previously. So, for example, the animated character
Scooby-Doo appeared in "Scooby-Doo, Where Are You?," "Scooby-
Doo Movies," "Scooby-Doo/Dynomutt Hour," and "Scooby's Laff-a-

Lympics." "Tom and Jerry" and "Grape Ape" became "Tom and
Jerry/Grape Ape." "Space Ghost" and "Frankenstein Jr." became
"Space Ghost/Frankenstein." "Superman," "Batman," and "Aqua-
man" were variously packaged in "Batman/Superman," "Superman/
Aquaman," "Super Friends," "The New Adventures of Batman," and
"The New Super Friends Hour." "Shazam!" was also seen in "The
Shazam!/Isis Hour," which ultimately split to become just "The Se-
crets of Isis."

The 1970s, then, marked the regular use of children's series
and their characters as essentially modular units that could be switched
around under umbrella titles and interlinked in many combinations.
By 1978 frequent use of this approach combined with the resurgence
of action-adventure and comic-chase plot lines to create a program
environment in which several related and unrelated action series
merged into one another during the primary children's block, under
a few umbrella titles. Both Appendix C, which presents all programs
aired in 1978, and Figure 4.1, which reviews the schedule for a particular Saturday in January of that year, bear witness to this development.

For example, 16 of the 24 Saturday morning series telecast during 1978 had been repackaged in one way or another. Moreover, six
of those 16 combined various action-filled segments under umbrella
titles that stretched across an hour or more. Thus, "The New Super
Friends Hour," "Batman/Tarzan," "Bugs Bunny/Road Runner,"
"Godzilla Power Hour," "Krofft Supershow 78," and "Scooby's Laff-a-
Lympics" enjoyed lengths that made them and their modular action segments stand out amont the typically half-hour Saturday morning fare.
"Scooby's Laff-a-Lympics" is a particularly interesting case, since
it linked action-adventure series to plot lines that the networks developed while they were avoiding action-adventures in the early and
mid-1970s. The program was the first two-hour Saturday morning
series, and it contained four unrelated segments. One was the well-
known series, "Scooby-Doo, Where Are You?," which used a "man
against supernatural" plot line. A second, "Captain Caveman and
the Teenangels," was an action-adventure about a fumbling prehistoric caveman and his helpers, three women reminiscent of the adult
"Charlie's Angels." A third segment was "Blue Falcon and Dynomutt," about a super crime fighter and his wacky dog. And the fourth
dealt with the "Laff-a-Lympics," a comic chase depicting Olympic-
like contests between the Yogi Yahoos, the Scooby Dooies, and evil
cheaters, the Rottens.

In the face of such fascinating changes and continuities in subject matter over the late 1960s, it may seem almost beside the point
to look at subject matter from other perspectives. And yet, asking
questions about fantasy/reality and time in these programs is worth-

while, since it provides still another window on diversity and still
more knowledge about the derivative, generally action-filled, and increasingly modular approach taken to subject matter by the end of the
decade. Actually, even the brief descriptions of series given in the
last few pages imply quite clearly that, in the 1970s, the networks continued to stress fantasy much more than reality and to emphasize "the
present" as strongly as before. It is true, though, that while the percentage of fantasy programs remained high, it fell in relation to the
figures for 1966-67 and 1968-69. From a high of 86 percent at the
end of the 1960s, fantasy programs dropped to 71 percent of the total
in 1970-71, 69 percent in 1974-75, and 62 percent in 1978. That drop
—and the associated rise of series based in reality to between 20 percent and 29 percent of the shows—can be related to several developments: the emergence of "man against nature" shows that plausibly
showed people confronting danger (for example, "Emergency plus
Four" and "Barrier Reef"), the development of situation comedies for
juveniles that revolved around plausible occurrences (for example,
"The Brady Kids" and "The Archie Show"), the emergence of realistic
problem dramas ("Afterschool Special" and "Fat Albert and the Cosby
Kids," for example), and the slight increase in nonfiction ("Watch Mr.
Wizard" and "In the News"). Interestingly, certain nonfiction shows
mixed fantasy and reality. For example, "Marshall Ephron's Illustrated, Simplified, and Painless Sunday School," "Make a Wish,"
and "Multiplication Rock" often used fantasy-based characters and
situations to teach religion, arithmetic, or the very distinction between fantasy and reality. As a result, the percentage of programs
clearly mixing fantasy and reality also rose over that of the late 1960s,
hovering between 6 percent and 12 percent of the total. Despite this
increase and the increase in programs based in reality alone, it ought
to be realized that, throughout the 1970s, the basic material in over
70 percent of network children's series contained strong elements of
fantasy.

The high percentage of fantasy programs and the plethora of adventure and situation comedy series among the nonfantasy fare mean
that programs focusing on the everyday joys and problems of children
were likely to be scarce. In fact, they were scarce, although not as
terribly rare as in earlier decades. The most consistently visible
programs of this type in the 1970s were the realistic problem dramas.
"The CBS Children's Film Festival" appeared weekly from 1970-71
onward, and "Fat Albert" followed, beginning in 1972-73. "Afterschool Special" started a monthly run in that year, and "Special Treat"
began its monthly run in 1976-77. "Muggsy" appeared weekly during
1976-77, and "Weekend Special," also a weekly show, came upon the
scene in 1978. A nonfiction program that voiced concerns of children
during 1972-73 was "Kid Talk," in which a panel of children discussed

contemporary issues. It was reminiscent of "Talk Around," which aired in 1952-53.

Reaching out directly to the home audience was as rare during the 1970s as it had been in the late 1960s. Only two programs, "Captain Kangaroo" and "Make a Wish," explicitly attempted to encourage children at home to take up craft making or other activities. Also infrequent were series even remotely involving ethnic or racial themes. In this case, however, the six programs telecast represented more ethnically or racially oriented shows than had aired during the previous 22 years combined. "Fat Albert and the Cosby Kids" dealt with black youngsters in a black neighborhood of North Philadelphia. "The CBS Children's Film Festival" presented generally realistic dramas about children from different countries. "Amazing Chan and the Chan Clan" told tales of the fictional Oriental detective and his brood. "I Am The Greatest" had black boxer Muhammed Ali helping good defeat evil. And "The Harlem Globetrotters" had the famous black basketball entertainers solving crimes, while "The Harlem Globetrotters Popcorn Machine" involved them in a fast-paced variety show.

Significantly, the two problem dramas among these shows—the ones most likely to genuinely introduce youngsters to other cultures—did not appear on Saturday morning. In fact, none of the realistic problem dramas that aired during the 1970s appeared in the primary children's block. As in the 1960s, prestige series tended to be removed from the center of marketing action. Therefore, Saturday morning fare tended to <u>accentuate</u> the major trends described earlier. It was more action-filled, fantasy-oriented, and present-oriented than programming as a whole. It also presented a higher percentage of "repackaged," "modular," and "umbrella" programs than did overall commercial network children's fare. Saturday morning also tended to air a lower percentage of nonfiction series than did all time slots taken together, but here the difference was a lot narrower than in the late 1960s—due to "In the Know," "In the News," "Multigrammar Rock," "Multiplication Rock," and "Schoolhouse Rock." Throughout much of the decade, at least two of those five-minute information spots scattered nonfiction material among the fictional fare on Saturday morning.

Characterization

The differences and similarities in subject matter between the 1970s and the late 1960s reverberated through differences and similarities in characterization. A comparison of Tables 4.5 and 3.8 reveals that the decrease in fantasy after the turn of the decade was associated with a decrease in humanlike animal protagonists, an increase

TABLE 4.5

Nature of Continuing Characters, 1970-78
(in percent)

| | 1970-71 (N = 58) | 1972-73 (N = 62) | 1974-75 (N = 55) | 1976-77 (N = 56) | 1978 (N = 43) |
|---|---|---|---|---|---|
| Human | 40 | 48 | 51 | 47 | 33 |
| Animal | 3 | 3 | 0 | 0 | 0 |
| Anthropomorphic animal | 14 | 14 | 6 | 7 | 12 |
| Anthropomorphic inanimate | 3 | 0 | 2 | 0 | 0 |
| Human and anthropomorphic | 26 | 21 | 20 | 27 | 36 |
| Human and animal | 12 | 5 | 11 | 6 | 7 |
| Other | 0 | 2 | 2 | 4 | 2 |
| No continuing cast | 2 | 7 | 9 | 9 | 10 |
| Total | 100 | 100 | 101 | 100 | 100 |
| Diversity index | .264 | .302 | .325 | .312 | .268 |

Note: Totals greater than 100 percent are due to rounding error.

Source: Compiled by the author.

in continuing humans, and a decrease in the overall human/animal diversity index. The rise of the information spots and anthology programs, such as "Afterschool Special," resulted in a small, though consistent, presence of series with no continuing cast for the first time. And, in a different area of characterization, the strong drop in action-adventure shows at the decade's turn specifically led to a sharp drop in programs with the kind of action-adventure characters that drew the most controversy—superheroes. Series with superheadliners fell from 32 percent and 43 percent of the total in 1966-67 and 1968-69 to 16 percent in 1970-71 and 7 percent in 1972-73. However, though the proportion of action-adventures resurged strongly by 1978, superheroes did not come back to nearly the same level as before. By 1978 only 19 percent of overall series titles contained the names of superheroes. It should be noted that similar shifts occurred on Saturday morning alone. For example, while in 1968-69 superheroes headlined 54 percent of the Saturday morning programs, in 1970-71 and 1972-73 they headlined only 20 percent and 7 percent, respectively. During the second half of the decade, programs with superheroes in their titles rose to nearly 25 percent.

The reduction in anthropomorphic animal characters and superhero headliners should not be taken to mean a reversion to the portrayals of the 1950s. Rather, the 1970s experienced a moderate step back toward human characters with no superpowers. The percentages of title headliners with extraordinary strengths and the percentages of programs with humanlike animals or inanimate objects in the cast were always higher than those of the 1950s. In fact, 1978 saw a rise of programs mixing humans and anthropomorphic beings to a level (36 percent of the total) exceeding all two-year spans. While several of those combinations appeared in comic-chase programs (for example, "The Pink Panther," "Sylvester and Tweety," and "Daffy Duck"), several others brought a mix of the human and humanlike into the action-filled fight against evil. For example, "Godzilla Power Hour" portrayed the close bond between the anthropomorphic title character and human regulars; "Jabberjaw" had a drum-playing white shark assisting a group of teenagers to solve underwater crimes; "Dynomutt Dog Wonder" resembled a bumbling person when aiding the Blue Falcon; and "Fantastic Four" (resurrected from 1968-69) turned its own human characters into humanlike beings.

During the 1970s, gender was one area of characterization in which strong and consistent differences from previous decades were evident. The sex of the title character or host, almost always male in the 1950s and 1960s, changed sharply from 1970-71 through 1978. In the two-year spans before 1970, over 65 percent (often over 75 percent) of all series persistently featured male headliners. During the 1970s that percentage fell—from 66 percent in 1970-71 to 52 percent in 1972-73, 51 percent in 1974-75, 47 percent in 1976-77, and 43 percent in 1978. It is important to remember that the decline was not due to an increase in series with female headliners. Those shows remained at less than 8 percent of the total. What did change was the percentage of programs with no title characters or host and the percentage of programs with titles referring to both male and female characters. Programs without title characters or hosts characterized between 9 percent and 20 percent of the whole from 1948-49 through 1968-69, while, after 1970-71, they ranged from 24 percent to 35 percent of all shows. Titles referring to both male and female stars by name or in groups (for example, "Archie and Sabrina," "Shazam!/ Isis Hour," "Super Friends") also increased rather dramatically. From 1950-51 through 1968-69, such titles did not comprise more than 6 percent of the total. However, in 1970-71, they rose to 19 percent, then fluctuated from a high of 21 percent to a low of 15 percent through 1978.

When females became somewhat more important as headliners in the action-filled environment, they also received more prominence as children in the continuing cast. Here, too, shows with females alone were very rare, comprising less than 5 percent of the whole. However, programs with both boys and girls in the continuing cast rose sharply over the late 1960s—from 2 percent in 1968-69 to 29 percent in 1972-73 to 50 percent in 1976-77. This rise coincided with a drop in the percentage of shows with boys only (from 16 percent in 1968-69 to 7 percent in 1976-77) and with an even stronger decrease in the percentage of series with no continuing children at all (from 80 percent in 1968-69 to 20 percent in 1976-77). To some extent, the decrease reflected the inclusion of "calmer" programming during the period of the FCC inquiry (for example, "The Brady Kids," "The Jetsons," "Sigmund and the Sea Monsters," and "The Archie Show"). However, as the decade progressed, more and more action shows included boys and girls as well. Sometimes the children in such shows were quite young. For example, "Land of the Lost" and "Valley of the Dinosaurs" saw boys and girls under 13 trying to survive with their families. More often, older youngsters—teenagers, actually—appeared in adventure programs. "Speed Buggy," for example, depicted two teenage boys and a girl as they traveled cross-country in search of mysteries to solve with their humanlike car. "Scooby-Doo, Where Are You?" involved two teenage boys and two teenage girls traveling with their dog in search of supernatural mysteries. "Kids from C.A.P.E.R." told stories of a special police crime-fighting unit of teenagers. And, "Josie and the Pussycats in Outer Space" placed an all-female rock group with their male friends on unexplored planets to encounter and battle forces of evil. The greatest proportion of programs with youngsters of both sexes occurred in 1976-77. In 1978 programs without any children rose to 48 percent of the whole, and those with both boys and girls dropped to 28 percent. Nevertheless, that year still included more children in programs—and more children of both sexes—than any two-year span before 1974-75. The changes were particularly evident on Saturday morning.

Format

In moving from a discussion of characterization to one of format, specific Saturday morning trends must take on an even greater emphasis. For, in the 1970s, Saturday morning did not remain merely the major repository of children's series. Rather, it emerged as an arena in which particular approaches to program format meshed with the action-filled, derivative, modular approach to subject matter in such a way as to create a style for the children's block that was unlike that of any other time slot. Program segments interlocked with longer program forms, commercials, and information spots to create a patchwork of related material that made Saturday morning television seem increasingly like one long, mosaiclike show.

As in the late 1960s, the "limited" style of animation was the basic glue that connected much of the programming, although the glue was not as widespread in the 1970s as in 1966-67 and 1968-69. Pressure group complaints about too many cartoons probably influenced the decline of animation during the 1970s. Comparison of Table 4.6 with Table 3.6 indicates that use of animation alone declined from 86 percent of all programs in 1968-69 to 63 percent in 1972-73, 49 percent in 1976-77, and 59 percent in 1978. These changes helped lower the live-action/animation/puppetry diversity index in relation to the late 1960s. However, the index was still higher than its level in the

TABLE 4.6

Live Action/Animation/Puppetry in Children's Series, 1970-78
(in percent)

|  | 1970-71 (N = 58) | 1972-73 (N = 62) | 1974-75 (N = 55) | 1976-77 (N = 56) | 1978 (N = 43) |
|---|---|---|---|---|---|
| Live action | 15 | 29 | 26 | 40 | 29 |
| Puppetry | 0 | 0 | 0 | 0 | 0 |
| Animation | 79 | 63 | 69 | 49 | 59 |
| Live and puppetry | 2 | 2 | 2 | 2 | 2 |
| Live and animation | 0 | 3 | 2 | 7 | 5 |
| All three | 4 | 2 | 2 | 2 | 2 |
| Other | 0 | 0 | 0 | 0 | 2 |
| Total | 100 | 99 | 101 | 100 | 99 |
| Diversity index | .649 | .483 | .545 | .401 | .436 |

Note: Totals greater or less than 100 percent are due to rounding error.

Source: Compiled by the author.

late 1950s and early 1960s. No puppet show existed in the 1970s, and only "Captain Kangaroo" and "The Banana Splits" mixed all three forms. A small number of series did mix live action and animation. "Animals, Animals, Animals" had host Hal Linden presenting animated and live-action segments about different creatures; "Fat Albert and the Cosby Kids" had Bill Cosby wittily explicating themes and morals in the animated episodes; "Curiosity Shop" had a cast using sketches, cartoons, and live-action films to inquire into different aspects of the world; and "Uncle Croc's Block" tried to spoof old-time children's shows through a mixture of live-action and cartoon buffoonery. Puppetlike characters hosting cartoons appeared in "The Skatebirds." The only series that mixed live action with puppetry was "The CBS Children's Film Festival," where Kukla, Fran, and Ollie hosted the often live-action movies.

Of the seven programs just mentioned, only three ("The Skatebirds," "Banana Splits," and "Curiosity Shop") aired on Saturday morning. In the 1970s the primary children's block was a good deal less oriented to mixtures of live action, animation, and puppetry than was programming as a whole, and a good deal less oriented to live action alone. It was also more oriented to all-animated fare. True, live action did increase over the late 1960s. From 9 percent of Saturday morning fare in 1968-69 and 5 percent in 1970-71, live action rose slowly to 31 percent in 1976-77 before declining to 22 percent in 1978. From 1970-71 through 1974-75, 90 percent, 85 percent, and then 85 percent of all Saturday morning series were fully animated. The figure dropped to 60 percent in 1976-77 but rose to 78 percent in 1978. Looked at another way, programs with at least some animation ranged from 66 percent to 95 percent of the Saturday morning total throughout the decade and generally hovered around the 80 percent mark.

The networks approached using a host (or not using a host) in children's series of the 1970s in much the same way they approached using animation, live action, or puppetry. The format they had established as dominant in the late 1960s continued into the next decade. In 1968-69, 90 percent of all series for children had no hosts. During the next decade, unhosted shows comprised close to 80 percent and never fell below 71 percent. Among the small number of programs that had hosts, the widest choice of presentation formats aired during the years of the FCC's most active interest in children's television, from 1970-71 to 1974-75. In 1968-69 hosted programs used four presentation formats, as Table 3.7 indicated. Table 4.7 shows that, in 1970-71, hosted programs used five formats. In 1972-73 and 1974-75, they used seven; in 1976-77, three; and in 1978, two.

One quiz show appeared during those years. "Runaround," hosted by Paul Winchell, had two teams scrambling to answer ques-

TABLE 4.7

Presentation Methods on Children's Series, 1970-78

(in percent)

| | 1970-71 (N = 58) | 1972-73 (N = 62) | 1974-75 (N = 55) | 1976-77 (N = 56) | 1978 (N = 43) |
|---|---|---|---|---|---|
| Unhosted | | | | | |
| Single drama* or nonfiction | 58 | 63 | 70 | 67 | 55 |
| Several dramas or nonfiction | 22 | 11 | 6 | 11 | 16 |
| Hosted | | | | | |
| Host with gang, drama or nonfiction | 5 | 8 | 9 | 9 | 21 |
| Host without gang, drama or nonfiction | 10 | 7 | 7 | 11 | 8 |
| Talk show | 0 | 5 | 0 | 0 | 0 |
| Demonstration | 2 | 2 | 0 | 0 | 0 |
| Quiz show | 0 | 2 | 0 | 0 | 0 |
| Variety show (no regular drama) | 2 | 0 | 2 | 0 | 0 |
| Concert | 2 | 2 | 4 | 0 | 0 |
| Nonquiz competition | 0 | 2 | 0 | 2 | 0 |
| Other | 0 | 0 | 2 | 0 | 0 |
| Total | 101 | 102 | 99 | 100 | 100 |
| Diversity index | .398 | .424 | .509 | .428 | .379 |

*Drama includes any performance that tells a story, whether live or recorded, studio or nonstudio based.

Note: Totals greater or less than 100 percent are due to rounding error.

Source: Compiled by the author.

tions. A nonquiz show also aired. "Junior Almost Anything Goes" had Soupy Sales overseeing a two-team competition at unusual outdoor games. The decade saw three talk shows, all in 1972-73. In "Kid Talk," four regular child panelists and two guest celebrities discussed current issues; "Take a Giant Step" had a teenage host coordinating a discussion about personal and social matters among other teenagers; and "Talk to a Giant" had teenagers discussing various subjects with celebrities. The concert category included one program, "Young People's Concerts," until it was discontinued after 1974-75. The demonstration category included "Discovery" (1970-71), a resurrected "Watch Mr. Wizard" (1972-73), and "Hot Dog" (1970-71), which exhibited the construction and operation of everyday items in serious and comic fashion by regulars Jonathan Winters, Woody Allen, and Jo Anne Worley. Variety series that aired in the 1970s were "The Hudson Brothers Razzle Dazzle Comedy Show" and "The Harlem Globetrotters Popcorn Machine." Both appeared during 1974-75.

Most hosted formats of the 1970s were more general than the ones just mentioned. They simply had individuals introducing dramatic or nonfictional material. Hosts without gangs comprised from 7 percent to 11 percent of the total programs, slightly more than in the late 1960s. Hosts with gangs hovered around the 8 percent level of 1966-67 throughout most of the decade. However, in 1978, the proportion of series using hosts with gangs rose sharply to 21 percent. In order to understand the significance of this increase, it is important to realize that many of the emcees were animated characters. Nonanimated hosts (with or without gangs) tended to head series with performing activities or prestige shows—for example, "Captain Kangaroo," "Animals, Animals, Animals," "CBS Children's Film Festival," "Fat Albert and the Cosby Kids," and "Make a Wish." There were exceptions, of course. "The Skatebirds" and "The Banana Splits" were nonprestige, action-filled shows that did not have animated hosts. Generally, though, when ordinary children's programs used emcees, they were animated along with the rest of the content.

Such characters fulfilled an important function. They bridged various unrelated program segments and brought continuity to the proceedings. This had been Mighty Mouse's function as host of "Mighty Mouse Playhouse" back in the 1950s. This practice continued throughout the 1970s in "Bugs Bunny," "Daffy Duck," "Bugs Bunny/Road Runner," "U.S. of Archie," and others. The jump in number of hosts during 1978 was tied to the increase of fiction programs with unrelated segments. Several of those shows used hosts with gangs to bridge the segments. For example, "The Krofft Supershow 78" had an animated rock group, Captain Kool and the Kongs, linking the "Dr. Shrinker," "Electra Woman," and "Wonderbug" action-adventures carried in that hour. "Bang-Shang Lalapalooza" had Archie and his friends presenting jokes and trivia information between animated versions of the Archie comic books. And, in "The C. B. Bears," the bears hosted a 60-minute show containing their own action-adventures as well as other action-adventure and comic-chase cartoon series.

Significantly, only three programs with human hosts ("The Hudson Brothers Razzle Dazzle Comedy Show," "The Harlem Globetrotters Popcorn Machine," and "Runaround") appeared on Saturday morning during the entire decade. It is true that, throughout the decade, the overwhelming proportion of Saturday morning shows had no hosts at all. From 1970-71 through 1976-77, unhosted series comprised from 85 percent to 94 percent of Saturday morning's total. However, when programs in the primary children's block did have hosts, they were almost always animated characters presenting cartoons. In fact, the rise of hosted programs to 30 percent of the Saturday morning total in 1978 reflected the rise of programs with unrelated animated segments and the use of animated hosts to bridge them.

The dominance of fully animated shows means that most Saturday morning programming was of the "nonstudio" kind. Only "Runaround," "H. R. Pufnstuf," "Lidsville," and "Lost Saucer" were enacted entirely on studio sets. ("The Hudson Brothers Razzle Dazzle Comedy Show" and "The Harlem Globetrotters Popcorn Machine" often supplemented their indoor variety with outdoor clips.) This overwhelmingly nonstudio orientation extended to programming outside the primary children's block as well. Just five other programs from 1970 through 1978 were videotaped in a studio: "Young People's Concerts," "Kid Talk," "Talk to a Giant," "Take a Giant Step," and "Watch Mr. Wizard."

The use of nonstudio fare over studio fare, of animation over live action and puppetry, of nonhosted programs over hosted programs, and of animated hosts over live-action hosts provided the appropriate formats for presenting the action-filled material that dominated subject matter throughout the decade. Action-adventure, comic-chase, and man against nature plots could be executed most effectively outside a studio. Moreover, "limited animation" provided the most efficient way to transport characters to nonstudio locations while encouraging more movement (with more fantastic powers) over more landscapes than was financially possible with live action. Animation also helped "calmer" shows fit into the action-filled environment more easily than if they had been done live. Hosts, whose words might slow the action, were best dispensed with, unless needed to bridge various segments. If hosts were required, animated hosts fit best, since they were less likely than humans or puppetry to interfere with the pace.

These suggestions about the functions of program format for subject matter are especially applicable to Saturday morning. The primary children's block did see fewer superhero headliners during the 1970s than in 1966-67 and 1968-69, and its percentage of action-adventure did drop moderately during the years of the FCC inquiry. Nevertheless, action-filled cartoons on Saturday morning (with "man against nature" and "comic-chase" plots taking up much of the action-adventure slack) hovered around their level of the watershed late 1960s. At the same time, certain differences in the handling of subject matter and format combined to create a different "look" to the fare. The primary differences in subject matter related to the nonfiction information spot series and the modular fiction presentations. Throughout most of the 1970s, "In the Know" or "In the News" on CBS and "Multiplication Rock," "Multigrammar Rock," or "Schoolhouse Rock" on ABC were laced throughout the Saturday morning schedules, appearing as many as eight times. The spots were slotted between programs and between segments of programs and were themselves surrounded by commercials and network identification logos. ABC, from 1974 through 1976, used a "bumper" device throughout the morning schedule, proclaiming in animated, musical fashion that this was a "funshine Saturday on ABC."

This succession of spots might seem to form an essentially irrelevant clutter between shows. Actually, however, many of the programs themselves contained a succession of disconnected sequences. For example, "Archie's Funhouse," "Archie Comedy Hour," and other Archie-related stories inserted music and joke segments between portions of the story; the Riverdale High characters would tell one-liners or present songs. "Yogi's Space Race" dispersed comic action-adventure shorts ("The Galaxy Goof-ups") between cliff-hanging episodes of a comic-chase competition that pitted Yogi Bear against characters of those shorts. And, toward the end of the decade, "Super Friends" had one or another of its heroes presenting safety tips and reminding viewers that the show would return after some "messages."

In the programs just mentioned, the various segments shared characters, if not specific themes. Other series contained segments that bore no relationship to one another in character or theme. The most traditional examples of this kind of show were the comic chases compiled from old theatricals—for example, "The Bugs Bunny/Road Runner Show," "Daffy Duck," and "Sylvester and Tweety." With the advent of the "modular" approach to program packaging in the 1970s, programs with newer cartoons also began to combine unrelated sequences. An early example (1968-69 through 1970-71) was "The Banana Splits." That hour-long series, bracketed by the antics of its puppetlike title characters, dispensed ten-minute segments of a live-action series, "Danger Island," between full episodes of four animated series—"The Three Musketeers," "The Arabian Knights," "The Hill-

billy Bears," and "Micro Venture." Other programs that combined
unrelated segments under umbrella titles have already been described:
"Bang-Shang Lalapalooza," "C.B. Bears," "The Krofft Supershow
78," and "Scooby's Laff-a-Lympics." Another, "Godzilla Power
Hour," deserves note for its timing of the two action-adventure series
that made up the show. A "Godzilla" episode ran for 15 minutes,
ended in a cliff-hanger, and was followed (after commercials) by a
complete "Jana of the Jungle" episode, which, in turn, was followed
by completion of the "Godzilla" tale.

The number of umbrella titles covering different segments of
various lengths increased markedly by 1978. On all three networks,
these segments merged into commercial separators and commercials.
ABC and CBS also added information spots in the morning schedule.
Moreover, the majority of 1978's series repackaged old material and
characters under new titles, often linking unfamiliar segments with
familiar ones. What becomes quite clear is that Saturday morning
children's television did not remain the succession of competing half-
hour programs that it was in the 1960s. Rather, the various scheduling, subject, and format trends that emerged during the 1970s transformed each of the network schedules into one long program comprised
of mostly animated parts stitched together across half-hour boundaries.
On CBS and ABC, the information spots, distributed throughout the
schedule as they were, added a kind of continuity to the proceedings,
proclaiming ABC's "funshine Saturday" idea without actually saying it.

Since newspaper and magazine program guides are predicated
on the notion of a succession of discrete series, Chart 4.1's Saturday
morning schedule for January 1978, adapted from the New York Times,
does not really convey the flavor of what has been discussed. However,
remembering the various spots that surround the shows, and knowing
the various segments that are covered by the individual titles, makes
it possible to get some idea of the true program flow from the chart.
NBC had the least developed patchwork of the three networks, with
three discrete half hours in its schedule—the animated "I Am the
Greatest" preceding two live-action adventures, "Thunder" and "Search
and Rescue." Nevertheless, the networks two initial hours of Saturday morning programming did show evidence of an emerging patchwork, with the various parts of "The C.B. Bears" leading into an
hour of Archie-related segments under the "Super Witch" (that is, Sabrina) and "Bang-Shang Lalapalooza" titles. CBS's schedule more
clearly illustrated the movement toward continuous interplay of long
and short segments, despite its half-hour "Space Academy" from
11:30 to 12:00. From 8:00 A.M., various action-adventures hosted
by "The Skatebirds" led into 90 minutes of comic chase in "Bugs Bun-
ny/Road Runner," which in turn led into 60 minutes of "Batman/Tar-
zan" adventure. Some live-action commercials and the live-action

"In the News" spots (with animated logos) threaded through this over-whelmingly animated program environment. On ABC it was virtually all animation, except for some commercials. The network with the most developed program patchwork, ABC presented four hours of action material under three titles—"All New Super Friends Hour," "Scooby's Laff-a-Lympics," and Krofft Supershow 78"—interlaced with the fully animated "Schoolhouse Rock."

## THE SHAPE OF PROGRAMMING

The video mosaic that ABC, CBS, and NBC were creating in their primary children's block by the late 1970s certainly formed the most dramatic difference between that decade and the late 1960s. Smaller differences were seen as well. More youngsters of both sexes and more shows with ethnic or racial themes appeared. The over-whelming domination of animated, action-filled fantasies relaxed just enough to allow the emergence of some calmer programming, some live-action programming, and some series dealing with the realistic problems of children. Significantly, though, the only shows generally embodying all these unusual characteristics were anthology programs telecast outside the Saturday morning marketplace. Two ("After-school Special" and "Special Treat") aired on a monthly rather than weekly basis. The live-action shows the networks televised on Saturday morning were action-filled "man against nature" series with pace and plot line that fit the established mold. Similarly, the "calmer" Saturday morning series were often animated versions of popular comic books or situation comedies designed for families that were known to attract large child audiences in syndication. Moreover, while a few nonfiction series became year-to-year Saturday morning fixtures for the first time, they took up no more than five minutes at a clip. They were short "reality breaks" on a fantasy-based mosaic.

The information spots may well have attracted more child attention than past nonfiction and thus have contributed to children's learning.[20] At the same time, there is the possibility that, because of their brevity, the spots could not explore subjects in a depth sufficient to foster creative understanding. It is interesting to consider the utility of the series for the networks, however. In the midst of a national debate about children's television, this novel format functioned as highly visible proof of increased "educational and informational programming" to parents, activists, and an aroused Federal Communications Commission. The use of Saturday morning heightened this visibility even more. At the same time, the information spots—since they were short, often animated, and bracketed by commercials—fit nonfiction as comfortably as possible into the flow of other Saturday programming so that audience flow from one half hour to another was not lost. In this manner, the networks could accrue benefits from the presentation of nonfiction while they were actually maintaining the amount of nonfiction programming at the traditionally low level.

Development of a program mosaic was a logical step beyond the development of information spots, only this time marketing rather than political utility seems to have been foremost. By combining and recombining segments with familiar and unfamiliar characters under new-sounding titles, by using 60- and 90-minute umbrella labels to hold together cliff-hanging and non-cliff-hanging segments, and by using information spots as elements of continuity in the morning schedule, the networks took their "audience flow" strategy a step beyond that of the 1960s. The children's block was closer than ever before to being one long program, with a patchwork program flow designed to keep the child viewer constantly anticipating, consistently flowing from one series to another—and, of course, from one commercial to another. In 1978 the "size" of this new program shape varied with each network. ABC had the largest, NBC the least-developed, mosaic. But, as this book has shown, children's television is an evolving form. The new shape contained within it a way to deal with political as well as economic pressures on the commercial networks. The shape made sense for the networks, and it was therefore likely to develop further.

NOTES

1. William Melody, Children's Television: The Economics of Exploitation (New Haven, Conn: Yale University Press, 1973), p. 88; and Barry Cole and Mal Oettinger, Reluctant Regulators (Reading, Mass.: Addison-Wesley, 1978), p. 250.

2. Cole and Oettinger, Reluctant Regulators, p. 249.

3. Ibid., pp. 254-55.

4. Ibid., pp. 276-84.

5. Federal Communications Commission, "Children's Television Programs: Report and Policy Statement," Federal Register 39 (November 6, 1974): 39397.

6. Cole and Oettinger, Reluctant Regulators, p. 280.

7. Federal Communications Commission, Television Programming for Children: A Report of the Children's Television Task Force (Washington, D.C.: Federal Communications Commission, 1979), vol. 1.

8. Melody, Children's Television, p. 87; and Federal Trade Commission, FTC Staff Report on Advertising to Children (Washington, D.C.: Federal Trade Commission, 1978).

9. Cole and Oettinger, Reluctant Regulators, p. 256.

10. Evelyn Sarson, ed., Action for Children's Television (New York: Avon, 1971).

11. Evelyn Kaye, ed., The Family Guide to Children's Television (New York: Pantheon, 1974), pp. 156-58.

12. "Petitioners Win Skirmishes, Wait for FCC Decision in Challenge to KTTV License," Better Radio and Television 13 (Winter 1973): 1.

13. "Commercial Network Children's Shows and Selected Syndicated Programs," Better Radio and Television 17 (Winter 1977): 3-11.

14. Federal Trade Commission, Advertising to Children.

15. Melody, Children's Television, p. 9.

16. Cole and Oettinger, Reluctant Regulators, p. 258.

17. Ibid.

18. Ibid., pp. 257-58.

19. Alan Pearce, The Economics of Network Children's Television Programming (Washington, D.C.: Federal Communications Commission, 1972).

20. Charles Atkin and Walter Ganz, "Children and Television News," Public Opinion Quarterly 42 (Summer 1978): 183-98.

# 5
## CONCLUSION: THE PRESENT
## AND THE FUTURE

The seasons that followed the 1978 television year saw an extension and elaboration of the Saturday program mosaic on all three networks. NBC began to air information spots—"Junior Hall of Fame," "Metric Marvels," "Time Out," and "Ask NBC News." CBS stuck with "In the News," and ABC, keeping "Schoolhouse Rock," added "Help!" a 60-second health spot, and "Dear Alex and Annie," a live-action advice spot. All three networks also had children's program producers interpolate health, safety, consumer, and other "instructional segments" directly into their already segmented Saturday series. Examples from 1980 can be drawn from NBC's 90-minute "Fred and Barney Meet the Shmoo," which combined "Flintstones" situation comedies with the "Shmoo's" comic action-adventures, and from ABC's "Plasticman," a 90-minute combination of "Plasticman" and "Mighty Man and Yuk" episodes. In the NBC show, the Shmoo (a Gumby-like character) regularly asked viewers to follow the bouncing ball in short sing-alongs. ABC's Plasticman presented consumer tips, often reminding viewers that sales slips protect their ability to return merchandise.

Umbrella titles continued to provide a coherence and flow to the video mosaic. Embraced by those 60-minute and 90-minute coverings, old and new children's series interlocked in modular fashion across what in the early 1970s had been traditional half-hour barriers. The norm in subject matter was still action-adventure and action-filled comedy, now peppered with short nonfiction pieces. Witness Variety's description of ABC's fall of 1981, Saturday morning lineup:

> The 8-9 a.m. slot will see the return of "The Superfriends Hour." At 9 a.m., the first half hour of "It's a Comedy Blockbuster" will lead off with the new Hanna-Barbera "Fonz and the Happy Days Gang." . . . Old kidvid stagers

119

"Scooby Doo and Scrappy Doo" will follow. But instead of mysteries, as in the past, they will be in several seven-minute comedy shows per segment. The last half hour will be occupied with the new "Richie Rich" from comic book land.

Ruby-Spears will program the next 90 minutes under the heading of "90 Minutes of Action and Comedy." One part of the first half-hour at 10:30 will feature the new cat character "Heathcliff" and the rest with a new dog character "Ding-bat." The second half-hour will go with the returning "Plasticman" in "The Plasticman Family." The last half-hour show, "Thundarr," a scifi cartoon. . . .

Interspersed within the schedule will be the five-minute segments of "Schoolhouse Rock," "Dear Alex and Annie" and the new "Dough Nut." The last-named is a consumer guide show aimed at youngsters. It is produced by Dahlia Productions. That company also produces "Help!," the 60-second health spots. There will also be four 30-second nutrition spots within each weekend sked.[1]

Chapter 4 suggested the utility the commercial networks derived from this "mosaic" approach to their main arena for children's programming. The interlocking pieces moving under 60- and 90-minute titles seem designed to maintain the child audience flow throughout the entire morning. Some of these pieces, the information spots, were visible evidence of "educational and informational programming" to the FCC and pressure groups but, at the same time (being short, often animated, and bracketed by commercials), fit nonfiction as comfortably as possible into the flow of other Saturday morning fare.

The purpose of this book has been to follow the development of this approach to children's television from commercial television's earliest days to the present. It happened in stages, through a complex mixture of changes in scheduling, subject matter, format, and characterization. While the primary focus has been on programming itself, the environment surrounding the production of children's television has been outlined, and influences affecting the direction and nature of programming have been explored. The findings support Cantor's contention that television programming is the result of a "negotiated struggle" between a number of groups, a struggle for control in which "some of those who participate . . . have more power in determining the content than others."[2] In network children's television, the dominant forces have clearly been the networks and their advertisers. While the particular nature of the relationship between the networks and the advertisers has changed over the past three decades, their basic goal regarding children's television has remained the same, namely, to bring an audience of youngsters to commercials on a cost-efficient basis. Government and public pressures have not blunted this goal. However, the strong criticisms from groups outside the industry in the early 1970s have had consequences. While they have been ineffective at changing basic programming criteria, they have eked out some concessions regarding increased diversity—slightly fewer action-adventure series, a few more live-action shows, a few more realistic dramas about children, more children of both sexes in the programs, and more visibility for nonfiction material.

Significantly, the most prestigious and substantial incarnations of these concessions have been programmed outside Saturday morning, where they could not interfere with the highly competitive attempts by the networks to manage audience flow through their schedules with time-tested, animated, action-filled material. Some of these ("Weekend Special" and "Thirty Minutes") have appeared on Saturday afternoons. More ("Afterschool Special," "Special Treat," and the fairly recent "CBS Playhouse" and "Razzmatazz") have aired on a less-than-weekly basis during weekday afternoons or during Sunday afternoons when sports have not been scheduled. At the same time, it is fascinating to consider that a different concession—the increased visibility of nonfiction material on Saturday morning through the information spots—sparked, or at least encouraged, the evolution of children's television toward a new shape, the video mosaic. Certainly, there is no evidence that ACT or other interest groups had this approach in mind when they urged more instructional programming. Of course, more research is needed on the specific reasons for programming changes of the 1970s. But the situation seems to indicate how difficult it is to predict the consequence of pressures upon complex organizational systems.

Opinions will differ on the meaning and desirability of the emerging video mosaic. Those who decried the lack of diversity in juvenile programming during the early 1970s will probably feel that the networks still have a long way to go in establishing a truly varied, meaningful schedule for children. At the same time, perhaps increased consideration should be given to the actual form of television that is developing on Saturday morning. It is a form that seems designed to attract youngsters to a particular network from early morning to early afternoon. One does not have to subscribe to an image of children as passive entities transfixed by the glimmering light of the home tube to feel that a flow of interlocking, sometimes cliff-hanging, programs could dissuade a substantial number of young people from leaving the television room, from talking a length with other family members, or from thinking creatively about "things to do." Remember that in recent years watching only two shows on Saturday morning has often meant watching 2.5 or more hours of programming. Moreover,

the bulk of Saturday morning network television time has been con-
sumed by animated fantasies. Very few (in most years, none) of the
programs (including the information spots) have urged youngsters
toward activities away from the sets. After all, such urging would be
counterproductive for the programmers. Their goal is to get the audience to remain to watch the commercials.

The problem of the video mosaic may also extend to the area that
some see as a future source of better, more varied children's television—cable-delivered satellite programming. In 1979 UA-Columbia
cable already provided a "Caliope" cable service aimed at children,
and the Warner-Amex cable boasted "Nickelodeon," an entire channel
that devoted 13 hours a day on weekdays and 14 hours a day on weekends to material for children. Caliope allowed local commercial in-
serts; Nickelodeon had none.[3] A trade advertisement for Nickelodeon
contended that "it's hearty, wholesome programming that will delight
PTAs, community groups, and just plain anxious parents . . . as
well as the kids."[4] Certainly, the fare both services provided stood
out as different from the run-of-the-mill network children's programming. Award-winning live-action and animated shorts adorned Caliope. Educational films and shows especially designated for particular
age groups were the pride of Nickelodeon. At the same time, it is interesting to note that at least two programs in the Nickelodeon lineup,
"Video Comic Books" and "Nickel Flicks," harked back to the earliest
days of network children's television, when the networks were search-
ing for available sources of low-cost programming. "Video Comics,"
described by the firm as "a unique new series . . . starring the kids'
favorite heroes like Green Lantern and Space Ranger (in a format
which enables them to read along)," seemed much like "Telecomics,"
"NBC Comics," and "Cartoon Teletales" of the very early 1950s.
"Nickel Flicks," described as "adventure serials from the golden days
of 'continued next week,'" recalled several programs from the 1950s
(for example, "Commando Cody," "The Gabby Hayes Show," "Cactus
Jim," "Bar 5 Ranch," and "Andy's Gang") that recycled old serials or
full-length films.[5]

Echoes such as these suggest that cable television for children
is passing through its own "promotional era," much like network children's programming did in its early days. It is possible that derivative, cost-efficient programming will become more the rule than the
exception as children's channels on cable become an accepted part of
the basic service. Nor is it too difficult to imagine how a children's
cable channel could become one long mixture of old and new animated
and live-action shorts designed to hold children to the set for hours at
a time. Even without pressures from advertisers to provide an audience for commercials, cable managers might feel pressure to justify
the existence of channels to their firms by pointing to the high use of

their setup and its relatively low cost. If commercials are introduced in one form or another, it is particularly easy to see how and why a video mosaic for children's cable could develop on a daily basis.

Remedies to this situation are easy to suggest but hard to implement. The difficulty of determining the consequence of pressures upon a complex organizational system often condemns the most clear-sighted efforts of government and interest groups to failure. Certainly, to be most effective, the efforts must be formulated with as much awareness as possible regarding the organizations involved, their history, industrial environment, and the primary reward systems that motivate their activities. But such awareness might result in a realization of the substantial institutional changes that are necessary to bring about certain fundamental alterations in programming aims. Deep-rooted institutional arrangements and policies are generally difficult, if not impossible, to dismiss. And yet, the forces that make network broadcast approaches to children so difficult to alter are only beginning to develop in the cable television, satellite, videodisc, and videotape arenas. It is here that the largest potential exists to shape public and private policy to suit the needs of U.S. children and parents. Basic questions should be formulated, aired, and discussed at many levels of society. For example, how much cable programming for children is desirable? How should cable channels for children be set up? Indeed, should they exist, or might juvenile material be better placed near programming for other groups (the elderly, ethnics, and so forth) to prevent an undesired "video mosaic" from developing? Should commercials be carried on cable programming for children?

Such questions should not be asked in a vacuum. Awareness of current technological, economic, and organizational issues relating to programming is essential. So is awareness of the history of television programming for children, its diversity and shape. For, in the case of children's programming, if the public chooses not to remember the past, it may very well be condemned to repeat it.


NOTES

1. "ABC Kidvid Asked for Next Fall: 'People' Cut, Cartoons Added," Variety, April 16, 1980, p. 30.

2. Muriel Cantor, "The Politics of Popular Drama," Communication Research 6 (October 1979): 389.

3. Marilynne R. Rudick, "Children's Television: Alternative Media and Technologies," in Television Programming for Children: A Report of the Children's Television Task Force (Washington, D.C.: Federal Communications Commission, 1979), 5:59-61.

4. Ibid., 5:115.

5. Ibid.

# APPENDIX A

## PROCEDURES USED IN THE STUDY

In establishing the sample of programs for this investigation of commercial network children's series, 1948–78, we had to define carefully a term ordinarily taken for granted—children's series. Since the major goal of the investigation was to examine trends in network programming aimed at children, we thought it logical to designate as children's shows those programs that the three commercial networks (ABC, CBS, and NBC) themselves designated as children's shows during the past 31 years. We defined series as programs that appear on a regular, though not necessarily weekly, basis. Note that programs without continuing casts, such as "Afterschool Special," and even information spots, such as "Schoolhouse Rock," come under this definition.

We obtained our list of series from two sources—Anthony Maltese's thorough catalog of network children's series (covering the years 1948–64)[1] and Nielsen rating reports on network programs (available beginning with the 1958 volume). All the programs listed in the Maltese study were included, since Maltese's definition of children's series paralleled our own. Given wide-ranging access to network files and publicity releases, he considered a program a children's show if network literature indicated it was produced on a regular basis especially for youngsters 12 years old or under. Fortunately, the Nielsen ratings also allowed us to determine the programs ABC, CBS, and NBC designed specifically for juveniles. Program classification codes, chosen by the networks, accompany each listing in the Nielsen report, and specific codes are used to indicate children's fare. Our only deviation from these codes was to include regularly scheduled information spots that were labeled "instructional/advice" in the Nielsen reports but, falling as they did between or within other children's series, were clearly intended for juveniles.

The fact that no contradictions appeared between the Maltese and Nielsen sources for the overlapping years 1958–64 gives credence to the reliability and validity of the sources. Checks on Maltese's de-

---

We would like to thank the A. C. Nielsen Company for permission to use the Nielsen Television Index Reports. Thanks are also due to the Television Information Office Library, the repository of those ratings, for providing a friendly environment in which to work.

scriptions of the programs—and descriptions of the programs shown
during the 14 years not covered by Maltese—were found in four other
references: Vincent Terrace's Complete Encyclopedia of Television
Programs, Nina Davis's annual listing of television shows, TV Guide,
and the New York Times. [2] The Maltese thesis and the Nielsen ratings
also provided sponsorship information. Particulars of program time,
day, and duration listed in the Maltese work were corroborated
through an examination of program schedules of the network flagship
stations as reported in the New York Times. We gathered this material in preparation for coding specific information about the children's
series of three decades. Appendix C lists the 405 children's series
that appeared on commercial network television from 1948 through
1978.

Our intention was to chart the range of choice offered in various
areas of programming: scheduling and program duration, subject
matter, format, and characterization. We developed a coding instrument that allowed us to plumb various facets of these characteristics
as well as to tap sponsorship information for every program. That
instrument is found in Appendix B, and much of it is self-explanatory.
Nevertheless, it might be useful to review some of the terms used.

The characteristics noted in the marking scheme are designated
by column numbers, a procedure that allows the most efficient trans-
fer of the data to a computer. Two coders, handling different programs, used the instrument. After writing the name and preselected
number of a show, a coder marked the network on which the program
appeared. If a show appeared on more than one network, it was
treated as a different show for each network and given more than one
number. The coder would next note the time length of the program
and the number of years it remained on the air. Then came a notation
of the specific years the program was on the air and the time periods
(morning, afternoon, early evening, and prime time) it filled during
those years. For reasons of efficiency, the programs were entered
in two-year periods. Thus, for example, a program televised on
Saturday morning in 1957 and Sunday morning in 1958 was 17 (that is,
Saturday morning) in columns 16-17 (designating couplet 1956-57) and
21 (that is, Sunday morning) in columns 18-19 (designating couplet
1958-59). In the fairly unusual case that a program changed time periods within a couplet, the time period it held longest was coded. In
cases of equal time duration, the first time period was used.

Each coder used the concept of a "television year" in marking
the couplets. Taking into account the longtime tendency for the new
network season to begin in September, the coder considered a television year as beginning in September and ending in August. For example, a program beginning in October 1977 was listed as part of the
1978 television year. A coder completed culling information about

scheduling and program duration by noting the number of times the show was televised in a week and then proceeded to a series of questions related to subject matter (columns 41, 45-46, 47-48, 49-50, 54, and 56), presentation mode (columns 42 and 43-44), and character portrayal (51, 52, 53, and 55). In the case of "minority racial orientation" and "minority ethnic orientation," a show was coded as having those qualities only if the racial or ethnic atmosphere reflected in the character depictions was a central aspect of the show. Many of the main subject categories are quite straightforward and self-explanatory. Here, however, is the specific meaning we attributed to each of them:

Storybook: Program emphasizing traditional fairylike tales and legends.

Western: Adventure having a U.S. frontier locale.

Science fiction: Adventure taking place in the future and focusing on technologies or social organizations that do not now exist.

Jungle or "wilds": Adventure taking place in a jungle setting or non-U.S. wilderness.

Police or law agent: Adventure that is not a western, science fiction, or jungle program and that focuses on a hero (or heroes) bringing evildoers to justice.

Nonpolice adventure: Adventure that does not fit into the above categories and that follows an individual character or group week after week.

Adventure in different settings: Program that has full-length adventures with different characters in different locations week after week.

Film with no thread: Program that presents several unrelated adventures in one program.

Realistic program drama: Drama that focuses on the realistic, everyday problems of a child or children. This category is applicable even if a program might have otherwise fallen into another category—as long as the focus is on the realistic, everyday problems of a child. No action-adventures series (in which the hero is consistently involved in an action-filled struggle against evil) can fit this category.

ABCs, arithmetic: Series dealing with ABCs and/or arithmetic.

Nature: Program emphasizing understanding of our natural surroundings—horticulture, zoology, and the like.

Other physical science: Program dealing with science but not emphasizing nature alone.

Occupation: Program specifically focusing on people's jobs.

Geography: Program focusing on contemporary peoples and places.

History: Series that enacts (accurately) or discusses historical events but does not stress biography.

Biography: Series that specifically presents biographies of individuals, past or present.

Religion: Program that discusses the customs and beliefs of world religions.

Mixture of nonfiction: Series that consistently combines the above subjects.

Sports: Recognized athletic competitions.

Competitive game: Team or individual competition not falling into the "sports" category.

Magic: Series focusing on the performance of magic.

Music: Series focusing on the performance of music.

Variety of performance: Program mixing the above categories. Such shows may include dramatic segments.

Subject mixture: Program that clearly mixes several of the above types.

Assigning categories to particular shows was quite a straightforward process; the labels were not difficult or ambiguous. However, before conducting the research, the coders (both graduate students) and I reviewed the meaning of the various categories and did practice runs together on several shows. The coders were then presented with descriptions of the same ten programs and asked to fill out coding sheets regarding each show. An accepted index of reliability, Scott's pi, was then calculated (percent of observed agreement - percent of expected agreement/1-percent of expected agreement), and the coding was found to be reliable (.89).[3] The data thus collected were then analyzed systematically. Literature on children's television, and on the general history, economics, and organization of the broadcast industry, was used to help place the material in perspective and draw out its implications.

NOTES

1. Anthony M. Maltese, "A Descriptive Study of Children's Programming on Major American Television Networks from 1950 through 1964" (Ph.D. diss., Ohio University, 1967).

2. Vincent Terrace, Complete Encyclopedia of Television Programs (South Brunswick, N.J.: A. S. Barnes, 1976 and 1979); and Nina Davis, ed. and comp., The TV Season (Phoenix, Ariz.: Oryx Press, annually since 1976).

3. See Oli Holsti, Content Analysis for the Social Sciences and Humanities (Reading, Mass.: Addison-Wesley, 1969).

# APPENDIX B

## CODING INSTRUMENT/TELEVISION
## TREND SURVEY

<u>Columns</u>

1-3.     Name of show

4.        Network

      1) ABC
      2) CBS
      3) NBC

5.        Time length of program

      1) Less than 15 minutes
      2) 15 minutes
      3) Half hour
      4) One hour
      5) More than one hour
      6) Other

6-7.     Number of years on television (to nearest year): _____

Columns 8-39 will deal with <u>specific years on the air</u>. Code the following variables with one of the following categories. Time indicates starting time. For shows with different slots, note slot of longest duration.

      00) Not on those years
      01) Monday through Friday    Morning (7:00-11:30)
      02)                               Afternoon (12:00 noon-4:00)
      03)                               Early evening (4:30-7:00)
      04)                               Prime time (7:00 P.M. -    )
      05) Friday alone               Morning
      06)                               Afternoon
      07)                               Early evening
      08)                               Prime time
      09) Any weekday but Friday   Morning
      10)                               Afternoon
      11)                               Early evening
      12)                               Prime time
      13) Multiple weekday (but
            not M-F)                Morning

| | | |
|---|---|---|
| 14) | | Afternoon |
| 15) | | Early evening |
| 16) | | Prime time |
| 17) | Saturday | Morning |
| 18) | | Afternoon |
| 19) | | Early evening |
| 20) | | Prime time |
| 21) | Sunday | Morning |
| 22) | | Afternoon |
| 23) | | Early evening |
| 24) | | Prime time |
| 25) | One weekday and Saturday | Morning/morning |
| 26) | | Evening/morning |
| 27) | | Other time combination |
| 28) | One weekday and Sunday | Morning/morning |
| 29) | | Evening/morning |
| 30) | | Other time combination |
| 31) | Multiple weekday and Saturday | Morning/morning |
| 32) | | Evening/morning |
| 33) | | Other time combination |
| 34) | Multiple weekday and Sunday | Morning/morning |
| 35) | | Evening/morning |
| 36) | | Other time combination |
| 37) | Saturday and Sunday | Morning/morning |
| 38) | | Evening/morning |
| 39) | | Other time combination |

| | |
|---|---|
| 8–9. | 1948–49 _____ |
| 10–11. | 1950–51 _____ |
| 12–13. | 1952–53 _____ |
| 14–15. | 1954–55 _____ |
| 16–17. | 1956–57 _____ |
| 18–19. | 1958–59 _____ |
| 20–21. | 1960–61 _____ |
| 22–23. | 1962–63 _____ |
| 24–25. | 1964–65 _____ |
| 26–27. | 1966–67 _____ |
| 28–29. | 1968–69 _____ |
| 30–31. | 1970–71 _____ |
| 32–33. | 1972–73 _____ |
| 34–35. | 1974–75 _____ |
| 36–37. | 1976–77 _____ |
| 38–39. | 1978– _____ |

40.     At most, how often is the show on in a week?

    1) Less than once
    2) Once
    3) Twice
    4) Three times
    5) Four times
    6) Five times
    7) Six times
    8) Seven times

41.     What type of show is it?

    1) A series shown at least weekly
    2) A special, nonholiday
    3) A nonweekly series
    4) Christmas special
    5) Easter special
    6) Thanksgiving special

42.     Does the show utilize live-action, puppets, or animation?

    1) Live action
    2) Puppets
    3) Animation
    4) Mixed live and puppets
    5) Mixed live and animation
    6) All three
    7) Other (write in)

43-44.  What is the presentation format of the show?

    01) No host—single drama, film, or cartoon
    02) No host—more than one film or cartoon
    03) Host with "gang" presenting films or cartoons or puppetry
    04) Host without "gang" presenting films or cartoons or puppetry
    05) Talk show
    06) Demonstration show
    07) Quiz show
    08) Variety show/circus
    09) Concert
    10) Nonquiz competition
    11) Other

45-46.  What is the main subject of the show?

    01) Fairy tales, "storybook"
    02) Western adventure or mystery
    03) Police or crime adventure
    04) Science fiction/space mystery or adventure

05) Jungle adventure or adventure in the wild
06) Adventure in nonpolice settings
07) Adventure in different settings
08) Story that focuses on the realistic problems of a child
09) ABCs, arithmetic
10) History
11) Geography and social studies, travel
12) Archeology
13) Astronomy
14) Nature and animals
15) Other physical science
16) Occupations
17) Biography
18) Religion
19) General mixture of nonfiction
20) Child sports
21) Adult sports
22) Competitive games
23) Craft and art lessons
24) Magic
25) Music
26) Variety of different performances
27) Several films or cartoons with no common thread
28) Strong mixture of above categories (note)
29) Other

47. What is the fantasy/reality nature of the show?

1) Predominantly reality
2) Predominantly fantasy
3) Well mixed

48. What is the time orientation of the show?

1) Present
2) Historical past
3) Prehistoric or mythical past
4) Future
5) Mixed
6) Unclear

49. Does the show have a minority racial orientation?

1) No
2) Black
3) Other

50. Does the show have an ethnic orientation?

1) Yes
2) No

51.     Are the continuing characters on the show human or animal?

  1) Humans
  2) Animals
  3) Anthropomorphic animals
  4) Anthropomorphic inanimate objects or nonanimals
  5) Human and anthropomorphic animals or nonanimals
  6) Human and animal
  7) Other
  8) There are no continuing characters

52.     Is the host and/or title character male or female?

  1) Male
  2) Female
  3) Both
  4) There is no host or title character
  5) Unclear

53.     Is the title character endowed with superpowers?

  1) Yes
  2) No
  3) Not applicable

54.     What is the clearest source for the show's main character or
        the show title?

  1) It seems original
  2) Radio
  3) Movies
  4) Comics
  5) Other television shows
  6) Mixture of media
  7) Books
  8) Other
  9) Not applicable

55.     Are the children in the continuing cast male or female?

  1) Male
  2) Female
  3) Both
  4) There are no children in the continuing cast
  5) Not applicable

56.     Does the show explicitly attempt to involve youngsters at
        home?

  1) Yes
  2) No

57.     What is the form of sponsorship?

   1) Full (or cooperating)
   2) Participating
   3) Sustaining
   4) Initially sustaining, later full
   5) Sometimes sustaining, sometimes participating
   6) Initially full, later participating
   7) Other
   8) Cosponsor
   9) Initially cosponsor, later participating

If the show has full or cooperating sponsors, list products. Regarding the product variables, note the most applicable of the following categories:

   1) Not a full sponsor (participating)
   2) Sole sponsor for run of the show
   3) Among the show's full sponsors

List sponsors, if full or cooperating

58.     Cereal firms_____
59.     Cookie firms_____
60.     Candies, chewing gum firms_____
61.     Bread firms_____
62.     Nonsoda beverage firms, soup companies_____
63.     Soda firms_____
64.     Multiple-product food companies_____
65.     Fast-food outlets_____
66.     Shoe firms, wallets_____
67.     Toy companies_____
68.     Soap and detergent firms_____
69.     Pen and stationery firms_____
70.     Pet food firms_____
71.     Meat companies_____
72.     Drug companies (for vitamins)_____
73.     Car companies, oil companies_____
74.     Insurance companies_____
75.     Peanut butter companies_____
76.     Beauty-product companies_____
77.     Tire companies_____
78.     Clothes companies_____
79.     Book or magazine companies_____
80.     Other_____

# APPENDIX C

## NETWORK CHILDREN'S SERIES, 1948-1978

### ALPHABETICAL LISTING

## LISTING BY TWO-YEAR PERIODS

An asterisk next to a program's title signifies the show aired on Saturday morning.

### 1948-49

Children's Sketchbook
Chuck Wagon
Hopalong Cassidy
Howdy Doody
Judy Splinters
Kukla, Fran, and Ollie
Lucky Pup
Mr. I Magination
Singing Lady, The
Super Circus

### 1950-51

*Acrobat Ranch
*Bar 5 Ranch
 Big Top, The
 Billy Boone and Cousin Kibb
 Buck Rogers in the 25th Century
 Buffalo Billy Show, The
 Buster Brown TV Show with
   Smilin' Ed McConnell and the
   Buster Brown Gang, The
 Cactus Jim
 Cartoon Teletales
 Chester the Pup
 Children's Sketchbook
 Chuck Wagon
 Cowboy Playhouse
 Cowboys and Injuns
*Foodini the Great
 Gabby Hayes Show, The

Gene Autry Show, The
Hold 'Er Newt
Hollywood Jr. Circus
Hopalong Cassidy
Howdy Doody
It's Fun to Know
Judy Splinters
Kid Gloves
Kukla, Fran, and Ollie
Life with Snarky Parker
Lone Ranger, The, (ABC)
Lucky Pup
Magic Slate
Mary Hartline Show, The
Mr. I Magination
Mr. Magic
Ozmoe
Paddy the Pelican
Panhandle Pete and Jennifer
Ranger Joe (ABC)
*Rootie Kazootie (NBC)
Sandy Strong
Singing Lady, The
Space Patrol
Super Circus
Telecomics, The
Tom Corbett, Space Cadet (ABC)
Tom Corbett, Space Cadet (CBS)
Tom Corbett, Space Cadet (NBC)
Versatile Varieties
Versatile Varieties, Junior Edition

Watch Mr. Wizard
Watch the World
*Your Pet Parade
Zoo Parade

1952-53

Atom Squad, The
*Bar 5 Ranch
Barker Bill's Cartoon Series
Big Top, The
Bil Baird Show
Cactus Jim
Ding Dong School
Gabby Hayes Show, The
Gene Autry Show, The
Hail the Champ
Hold 'Er Newt
*Hollywood Jr. Circus
Howdy Doody
In the Park
Junior High Jinks
*Junior Rodeo
Kukla, Fran, and Ollie
Lone Ranger, The, (ABC)
Lone Ranger, The, (CBS)
M&M's Candy Carnival
Magic Slate
Meet Me at the Zoo
Mr. I Magination
Once upon a Fence
Paddy the Pelican
*Pud's Prize Party
Ranger Joe (ABC)
Ranger Joe (CBS)
*Rod Brown of the Rocket Rangers
*Rootie Kazootie (ABC)
*Rootie Kazootie (NBC)
Roy Rogers Show, The
Sky King (ABC)
Sky King (NBC)
*Smilin' Ed McConnell and His Gang
  (ABC)
*Smilin' Ed McConnell and His Gang
  (CBS)

Space Patrol
Summer School
Super Circus
Tom Corbett, Space Cadet (ABC)
Tom Corbett, Space Cadet (NBC)
Tootsie Hippodrome
Watch Mr. Wizard
Whistling Wizard, The
*Winky Dink and You
Zoo Parade

1954-55

*Adventures of Champion, The
Adventures of Rin Tin Tin, The
*Animal Time
Atom Squad, The
Barker Bill's Cartoon Series
Big Top, The
Captain Gallant of the Foreign
  Legion
*Captain Kangaroo
*Captain Midnight
Cartoon Comedies
*Commando Cody
Contest Carnival
Ding Dong School
Excursion
Exploring God's World
*Funny Boners
Garfield Goose and Friends
Gene Autry Show, The
*Happy Felton's Spotlight Gang
Howdy Doody
Kukla, Fran, and Ollie (ABC)
Kukla, Fran, and Ollie (NBC)
Let's Take a Trip
Lone Ranger, The, (ABC)
Men of Tomorrow
Pinky Lee Show, The
*Rod Brown of the Rocket Rangers
Roy Rogers Show, The
Sky King (ABC)
*Smilin' Ed McConnell and His
  Gang (ABC)

Soupy Sales Show, The
*Space Patrol
Summer School
Super Circus
Tom Corbett, Space Cadet (NBC)
Tootsie Hippodrome
Uncle Johnny Coons (CBS)
Watch Mr. Wizard
Wild Bill Hickok (CBS)
Winky Dink and You
Zoo Parade

### 1956-57

Adventures of Rin Tin Tin, The
*Andy's Gang
Big Top, The
Boing Boing Show
Captain Gallant of the Foreign
  Legion
*Captain Kangaroo
*Captain Midnight
Cartoon Theatre (CBS)
*Children's Corner, The
Choose Up Sides
Circus Boy (NBC)
Cowboy Theater
Ding Dong School
*Fury
Gene Autry Show, The
Giant Step, The
*Gumby
Heckle and Jeckle Show, The,
  (CBS)
Howdy Doody
*It's a Hit
Kukla, Fran, and Ollie (ABC)
Let's Take a Trip
Lone Ranger, The, (ABC)
Mickey Mouse Club, The
*Mighty Mouse Playhouse, The
*Paul Winchell Show, The
Pinky Lee Show
Popsickle Five Playhouse
Roy Rogers Show, The
*Ruff and Ready Show, The

Sky King (ABC)
Super Circus
*Susan's Show
*Tales of the Texas Rangers
Talk Around
Watch Mr. Wizard
Wild Bill Hickok (ABC)
Wild Bill Hickok (CBS)
Winky Dink and You
Zoo Parade

### 1958-59

Adventures of Rin Tin Tin, The
*Andy's Gang
Boing Boing Show
*Captain Kangaroo
*Circus Boy (ABC)
*Fury (NBC)
*Heckle and Jeckle Show, The,
  (CBS)
*Howdy Doody
Kukla, Fran, and Ollie
Let's Take a Trip
Lone Ranger, The, (ABC)
Mickey Mouse Club, The
*Mighty Mouse Playhouse, The
Noah's Ark
Paul Winchell Show, The
*Ruff and Ready Show, The
Shirley Temple's Storybook
Sky King (CBS)
*Susan's Show
*Uncle Al Show, The
*Uncle Johnny Coons (NBC)
Walt Disney's Adventure Time
Watch Mr. Wizard
Wild Bill Hickok (ABC)
Wild Bill Hickok (CBS)
Woody Woodpecker Show, The
Young People's Concerts

### 1960-61

Adventures of Rin Tin Tin, The
Bugs Bunny Show, The
*Bullwinkle (NBC)

*Captain Kangaroo
*Circus Boy (NBC)
Expedition
*Fury
*Heckle and Jeckle Show, The,
   (CBS)
*Howdy Doody
*King Leonardo
Lone Ranger, The, (ABC)
*Lone Ranger, The, (NBC)
Lunch with Soupy Sales
*Magic Land of Allakazam, The,
   (CBS)
Matty's Funday Funnies
*Mighty Mouse Playhouse, The
My Friend Flicka (ABC)
*On Your Mark
One, Two Three—Go!
*Outside In
Paul Winchell Show, The
*Pip the Piper (ABC)
*Pip the Piper (NBC)
Rockey and His Friends
*Ruff and Ready Show, The
*Shari Lewis Show, The
Sky King (CBS)
*Video Village Junior
Watch Mr. Wizard
Young People's Concerts

## 1962-63

*Adventures of Rin Tin Tin, The
*Alvin Show, The
Beany and Cecil
Bugs Bunny Show, The
Bullwinkle (NBC)
Burr Tillstrom's Kukla, Fran,
   and Ollie
*Captain Kangaroo
Discovery
Expedition
Exploring
*Fury
*Hector Heathcote Show, The
*King Leonardo

Magic Land of Allakazam, The,
   (ABC)
*Magic Land of Allakazam, The,
   (CBS)
*Magic Midway
*Magic Ranch, The
Matty's Funday Funnies with
   Beany and Cecil
*Mighty Mouse Playhouse, The
My Friend Flicka
One, Two Three—Go!
*Pip the Piper (NBC)
Reading Room
*Shari Lewis Show, The
Sky King (CBS)
*Tennessee Tuxedo and His Tales
   (ABC)
*Video Village Junior
Watch Mr. Wizard
Young People's Concerts

## 1964-65

*Adventures of Rin Tin Tin, The,
   (CBS)
*Alvin Show, The
*Annie Oakley
Beany and Cecil
*Buffalo Bill, Jr.
Bugs Bunny Show, The
Bullwinkle (NBC)
CBS Children's Theater
*Captain Kangaroo
Discovery
Do You Know?
Exploring
*Fireball XL-5
*Fury
*Hector Heathcote Show, The
*Hoppity Hooper
*Jetsons, The, (ABC)
*Jetsons, The, (CBS)
*Linus the Lionhearted
Magic Land of Allakazam, The,
   (ABC)
*Mighty Mouse Playhouse, The

*Mr. Mayor
My Friend Flicka
*New Casper Cartoon Show, The
Porky Pig Show, The
*Quick Draw McGraw
Science All-Stars
*Shari Lewis Show, The
Shenanigans
*Tennessee Tuxedo and His Tales
 (ABC)
*Top Cat
Underdog (NBC)
Watch Mr. Wizard
Young People's Concerts

### 1966-67

Animal Secrets
*Atom Ant/Secret Squirrel Show,
 The
*Beagles, The, (CBS)
Beany and Cecil
*Beatles, The
Bugs Bunny Show, The
Bullwinkle (ABC)
Captain Kangaroo
*Cool McCool
Discovery
*Fireball XL-5
*Frankenstein Jr. and the Impossi-
 bles
*Fury
*Hoppity Hooper
Jetsons, The, (NBC)
*King Kong
*Linus the Lionhearted (ABC)
*Linus the Lionhearted (CBS)
*Magilla Gorilla Show, The
*Mighty Mouse and the Mighty
 Heroes
*Mighty Mouse Playhouse, The
Milton the Monster
Peter Potamus Show, The
*Porky Pig Show, The
*Quick Draw McGraw
Road Runner Show, The, (CBS)

*Secret Squirrel
*Space Ghost
*Space Kiddettes
*Super Six, The
*Superman
Tom and Jerry
Top Cat
*Underdog (CBS)
*Underdog (NBC)
Young People's Concerts
Zoorama

### 1968-69

Aquaman
*Adventures of Gulliver, The
*Animal World (CBS)
*Archie Show, The
*Atom Ant/Secret Squirrel Show,
 The
*Banana Splits Adventure Hour,
 The
*Batman/Superman Hour, The
Beagles, The, (ABC)
Beatles, The
*Birdman
*Bugs Bunny-Road Runner Hour
Bullwinkle (ABC)
*Captain Kangaroo
Cool McCool
Discovery
*Fantastic Four, The, (ABC)
*Fantastic Voyage
*Flintstones, The
*Frankenstein Jr.
*George of the Jungle
*Go Go Gophers, The
*Herculoids, The
*Jonny Quest (CBS)
*Journey to the Center of the Earth
*King Kong
*Linus the Lionhearted (ABC)
Linus the Lionhearted (CBS)
*Lone Ranger, The, (CBS)
Milton the Monster
*Moby Dick and the Mighty Mightor

*New Casper Cartoon Show, The
  Road Runner Show, The, (CBS)
*Samson and Goliath
*Shazzan!
*Space Ghost
*Spider-Man
  Storybook Squares, The
*Super President
*Super Six, The
*Superman/Aquaman Hour, The
*Tennessee Tuxedo
  Tom and Jerry
  Top Cat
  Underdog (CBS)
*Underdog (NBC)
*Wacky Races, The
*Young People's Concerts
*Young Samson

## 1970-71

*Adventures of Gulliver, The
  Animal World (CBS)
*Archie Comedy Hour, The
*Archie's Funhouse Featuring the
  Giant Joke Box
*Banana Splits Adventure Hour,
  The
*Batman
*Bugaloos, The
*Bugs Bunny-Road Runner Hour,
  The
  Bullwinkle (ABC)
  CBS Children's Film Festival,
  The
  Captain Kangaroo
*Cartoons
*Cattanooga Cats, The
*Dastardly and Muttley in Their
  Flying Machines
  Discovery
  Doctor Doolittle
  Dudley Do-Right Show, The
*Fantastic Four, The, (ABC)
*Fantastic Voyage
  Flintstones, The

George of the Jungle
*H. R. Pufnstuf (NBC)
*Hardy Boys, The
*Harlem Globetrotters, The
*Heckle and Jeckle Show, The,
  (NBC)
*Here Come the Double Deckers
*Here Comes the Grump
  Hot Dog
*Hot Wheels
*In the Know
*Jambo
  Jetsons, The, (CBS)
  Jonny Quest (ABC)
  Jonny Quest (CBS)
*Josie and the Pussycats
*Lancelot Link, Secret Chimp
  Monkees, The, (CBS)
*Motor Mouse
*New Casper Cartoon Show, The
*Perils of Penelope Pitstop, The
*Pink Panther Show, The
*Reluctant Dragon and Mr. Toad,
  The
*Sabrina and the Groovie Goolies
*Scooby-Doo, Where Are You?
*Skyhawks
*Smokey the Bear Show, The
*Spider-Man
  Superman
  Tom and Jerry
*Tomfoolery
  Underdog (NBC)
  Wacky Races, The
*Where's Huddles?
*Will the Real Jerry Lewis Please
  Sit Down
*Woody Woodpecker Show, The
  You Are There
  Young People's Concerts

## 1972-73

  Afterschool Special
*Amazing Chan and the Chan Clan,
  The

Archie's Funhouse Featuring the Giant Joke Box
*Archie's TV Funnies
Around the World in 80 Days
*Barkleys, The
*Barrier Reef
*Brady Kids, The
*Bugaloos, The
*Bugs Bunny Show, The
Bullwinkle (ABC)
CBS Children's Film Festival, The
Captain Kangaroo
*Curiosity Shop
*Deputy Dawg
Doctor Doolittle
Fat Albert and the Cosby Kids
*Flintstones Comedy Hour, The
*Funky Phantom
Groovie Goolies, The, (CBS)
*H. R. Pufnstuf (ABC)
*Harlem Globetrotters, The
*Help! It's the Hair Bear Bunch
Here Come the Double Deckers
*Houndcats, The
*In the News
*Jackson Five, The
Jetsons, The, (ABC)
*Jetsons, The, (NBC)
Jonny Quest (ABC)
*Josie and the Pussycats
*Josie and the Pussycats in Outer Space
*Kid Power
Kid Talk
Lancelot Link, Secret Chimp
*Lidsville
Make a Wish
Monkees, The, (ABC)
Monkees, The, (CBS)
*Multiplication Rock
*Osmonds, The
*Pebbles and Bamm Bamm
*Pink Panther Show, The
Reluctant Dragon and Mr. Toad, The

*Road Runner Show, The, (ABC)
*Roman Holidays
*Runaround
*Sabrina, the Teen-Age Witch
*Saturday Superstar Movie, The
*Scooby-Doo, Where Are You?
*Sealab 2020
*Smokey the Bear Show, The
*Take a Giant Step
Talk to a Giant
Tom and Jerry
*Underdog (NBC)
Watch Mr. Wizard
*Will the Real Jerry Lewis Please Sit Down
*Woody Woodpecker Show, The
Young People's Concerts

## 1974-75

*Addams Family, The
Afterschool Special
*Amazing Chan and the Chan Clan, The
*Bailey's Comets
*Brady Kids, The
*Butch Cassidy and the Sundance Kids
CBS Children's Film Festival, The
Captain Kangaroo
*Devlin
*Emergency plus Four
Everything's Archie
Family Classics Theatre
Fat Albert and the Cosby Kids
*Flintstones Show, The
Go
*Goober and the Ghost Chasers
H. R. Pufnstuf
*Harlem Globetrotters Popcorn Machine, The
Help! It's the Hair Bear Bunch
*Hong Kong Phooey
*Hudson Brothers Razzle Dazzle Comedy Show, The

*In the News
*Inch High Private Eye
*Jeannie
Jetsons, The, (NBC)
*Josie in Outer Space
Kid Power
*Korg: 70,000 B.C.
*Land of the Lost
*Lassie's Rescue Ranger
*Lidsville
Make a Wish
Marshall Ephron's Illustrated,
    Simplified and Painless Sunday
    School
*Mission Magic
*Multigrammar Rock
*My Favorite Martian
*New Adventures of Gilligan, The
Osmonds, The
*Partridge Family: 2200 A.D.,
    The
*Pink Panther Show, The
*Run, Joe, Run
Saturday Superstar Movie, The
*Scooby-Doo, Where Are You?
*Shazam!
*Sigmund and the Sea Monsters
*Speed Buggy (CBS)
*Star Trek
*Super Friends
*These Are the Days
U.S. of Archie, The
*Valley of the Dinosaurs
*Wheelie and the Chopper Bunch
*Yogi's Gang
Young People's Concerts

1976-77

Afterschool Special
*Animals, Animals, Animals
*Ark II
*Beyond the Planet of the Apes
*Big John, Little John
*Bugs Bunny-Road Runner Hour,
    The

CBS Children's Film Festival,
    The
Captain Kangaroo
*Clue Club
Devlin
*Emergency plus Four
*Far Out Space Nuts
Fat Albert and the Cosby Kids
Festival of the Lively Arts
*Ghost Busters, The
Go—USA
*Groovie Goolies, The, (ABC)
Harlem Globetrotters, The
*Hong Kong Phooey
*In the News
*Jabberjaw
Jetsons, The, (NBC)
*Josie and the Pussycats
Junior Almost Anything Goes
Kids from C.A.P.E.R., The
*Krofft Supershow, The
*Land of the Lost
*Lost Saucer, The
*McDuff, the Talking Dog
Make a Wish
Marshall Ephron's Illustrated,
    Simplified and Painless Sunday
    School
*Monster Squad, The
Muggsy
*New Adventures of Batman, The
*New Adventures of Gilligan, The
*Oddball Couple, The
*Pebbles and Bamm Bamm
*Pink Panther Show, The
*Run, Joe, Run
*Schoolhouse Rock
*Scooby-Doo/Dynomutt Hour, The
*Secret Lives of Waldo Kitty, The
*Shazam!—Isis Hour, The
*Sigmund and the Sea Monsters
*Space Ghost/Frankenstein
    Special Treat
*Speed Buggy (ABC)
*Super Friends

These Are the Days
*Tom and Jerry/Grape Ape Show, The
Uncle Croc's Block
U.S. of Archie, The
Valley of the Dinosaurs
Way Out Games
*Westwind to Hawaii

### 1978

Afterschool Special
Animals, Animals, Animals
*Archie and Sabrina
Ark II
Baggy Pants and the Nitwits
*Bang-Shang Lalapalooza Show, The
*Batman/Tarzan Adventure Hour, The
*Bugs Bunny-Road Runner Hour, The
*C.B. Bears, The
CBS Children's Film Festival, The
Captain Kangaroo
*Daffy Duck
*Dynomutt Dog Wonder
*Fantastic Four, The (NBC)
Fat Albert and the Cosby Kids
Festival of the Lively Arts

Ghost Busters, The
*Go Go Globetrotters
*Godzilla Power Hour
Great Grape Ape Show, The
*I Am the Greatest: The Adventures of Muhammad Ali
*In the News
Jabberjaw
*Krofft Supershow 78, The
*New Super Friends Hour, The
Oddball Couple, The
Red Hand Gang, The
*Schoolhouse Rock
*Scooby's All Star Laff-a-Lympics
*Search and Rescue: The Alpha Team
Secrets of Isis, The
Skatebirds, The
Space Academy
Space Sentinels
Special Treat
*Super Witch
*Sylvester and Tweety
*Think Pink Panther
*Three Robonic Stooges
*Thunder
Weekend Special
What's New Mr. Magoo
*Yogi's Space Race

# INDEX

Network Children's Series, 1948-78, are indexed in Appendix C, Alphabetical Listing.

# ABOUT THE AUTHOR

JOSEPH TUROW is Assistant Professor of Communication at Purdue University. Born in Brooklyn in 1950, he attended the University of Pennsylvania, receiving a B.A. in English and an M.A. and Ph.D. in communications. His articles on mass media organizations and mass media content have appeared in Journal of Communication, Journal of Broadcasting, Communication Research, Library Quarterly, Journal of Popular Culture, Public Opinion Quarterly, and elsewhere. In addition, he compiles a research notes column for Emmy: The Magazine of the Academy of Television Arts and Sciences. His previous book, Getting Books to Children: An Exploration of Publisher-Market Relations, was published in 1979.